—THE—
GREAT PYRAMID

HOAX

"Egyptologists consider the ochre-painted Khufu cartouche in the Great Pyramid as the ultimate proof that this pyramid belongs to the Fourth Dynasty pharaoh Khufu. But much controversy surrounds its authenticity. If the Khufu cartouche is indeed a hoax, then the implications are tremendous. Scott Creighton has undertaken a very bold and meticulous investigation into this mystery. *The Great Pyramid Hoax* is a must-read book for all seekers of truth."

ROBERT BAUVAL, AUTHOR OF *THE SOUL OF ANCIENT EGYPT*

"An intriguing narrative, *The Great Pyramid Hoax* expertly weaves its way through the sands of time, as it revisits one of Egyptology's most contentious issues—the dating of the Great Pyramid. In the best traditions of alternative research Creighton takes the reader on a personal journey of exploration, skillfully weaving powerful themes upon clear emotional expression, as he attempts to uncover the veracity behind one of Egypt's most endearing mysteries. A must-read for those searching for the truth."

LORRAINE EVANS, EGYPTOLOGIST, DEATH HISTORIAN, AND AUTHOR OF *KINGDOM OF THE ARK*

—THE—
GREAT PYRAMID
HOAX

The Conspiracy to Conceal the
True History of Ancient Egypt

SCOTT CREIGHTON

Bear & Company
Rochester, Vermont • Toronto, Canada

Bear & Company
One Park Street
Rochester, Vermont 05767
www.BearandCompanyBooks.com

Bear & Company is a division of Inner Traditions International

Library of Congress Cataloging-in-Publication Data
Names: Creighton, Scott, author.
Title: The Great Pyramid hoax : the conspiracy to conceal the true history of
    Ancient Egypt / Scott Creighton.
Description: Rochester, Vermont ; Toronto, Canada : Bear & Company, 2017. |
    Includes bibliographical references and index.
Identifiers: LCCN 2016018835 (print) | LCCN 2016021070 (e-book) |
    ISBN 9781591437895 (pbk.) | ISBN 9781591437901 (e-book)
Subjects: LCSH: Great Pyramid (Egypt) | Great Pyramid
    (Egypt)—History—Chronology. | Archaeological expeditions—Egypt—
    Jāizah—History—19th century. | Vyse, Richard William Howard, 1784–1853. |
    Egyptology—History—19th century.
Classification: LCC DT63 .C74 2017 (print) | LCC DT63 (e-book) |
    DDC 932/.01—dc23
LC record available at https://lccn.loc.gov/2016018835

Printed and bound in the Unite States by P. A. Hutchison Company

10 9 8 7 6 5 4 3 2 1

Text design and layout by Debbie Glogover
This book was typeset in Garamond Premier Pro with Futura Std and Gill Sans
MT Pro as display fonts

To send correspondence to the author of this book, mail a first-class letter to the
author c/o Inner Traditions • Bear & Company, One Park Street, Rochester, VT
05767, and we will forward the communication.

*For my wife, Louise, and my children,
Jamie and Nina . . . forever.*

CONTENTS

FOREWORD

Work in the field of archaeology is somewhat like prospecting for gold. Both are disciplines of discovery that require the utmost care, patience, and perseverance but only occasionally reward the practitioner with a substantive return. When archaeological studies do produce such a return, a correct understanding of the significance of a finding may require specialized knowledge or rest on subtleties of understanding that the typical layperson may not possess. This means that the average person may not always be competent to evaluate the claims of competing researchers. Meanwhile, truly productive finds are the stuff from which archaeological careers are molded, academic reputations fostered, and theoretical ground staked. Knowing this, it seems clear that professional researchers must be subject to ongoing motivation to produce such claims.

Likewise, Egyptology is a field in which a small number of professionals have historically exercised a high degree of control over such things as access to sites, distribution of financial resources, and publication of results. Great egos tend to flock to positions with this degree or quality of control. In such an environment, it seems inevitable that practitioners might sometimes be tempted to take personal advantage of their specialized knowledge or position and leverage it to influence a career-making claim.

Structures on the Giza plateau in Egypt represent the most obvious reference points by which a modern observer may infer the outlook and intentions of our ancient ancestors. Foremost among these (second only to the incomparable Sphinx) is the Great Pyramid, or Pyramid of Khufu. Its sheer size, central position on the Giza plateau, and structural precision serve as an open invitation to students of ancient mysteries to make it a focus of their attention. The call of the Great Pyramid is made even more enticing by the many uncertainties that attend this great edifice, coupled with the relative sparseness of evidence on which these uncertainties often rest. For example, theories abound in relation to how the pyramid may have been built, what practical functions it might have served in ancient times, what undiscovered hidden chambers it might potentially house, whether slaves or paid workers were enlisted to construct it, what special qualities of electricity or resonance its stone blocks might possess, and so on.

First among the mysteries of the Great Pyramid is the persistent question of who actually built it. To those of us who see likelihood in the existence of civilizations prior to ancient Egypt, there is a temptation to credit the Great Pyramid to some advanced culture now lost to the mists of time. However, from an academic perspective, the era of origin for the Great Pyramid is considered to be a closed question: the consensus is that it was commissioned by the second pharaoh of the Fourth Dynasty of Egypt, a king named Khufu who ruled circa 2550 BCE. However, some modern-day researchers express doubt about a viewpoint that casts as a royal tomb a structure that, to all outward evidences, never actually housed a pharaoh's body. We might be inclined to simply set this inconvenient circumstance aside if we were confident that the official viewpoint was upheld by other unshakable evidence. But as we shall see as this book progresses, such does not always seem to be the case.

Despite the often careful fieldwork that has historically been carried out by archaeologists, we could argue that there is a kind of myopia at work in the field of Egyptology that can limit official perspectives on the likely purposes of ancient structures. The prevailing mind-set is one from which we might imagine future archaeologists who explore cultures of the twenty-first century excavating "local temple complexes" and "palaces," where today one sees only strip malls and Home Depots. In the real world, expectation can influence outcome. It has been famously said that if we choose to consult a surgeon with a problem, we can reasonably expect to hear a surgical solution proposed. The same is true in fields like Egyptology, where despite the arguably ethical intentions of researchers, findings can be influenced by strong personalities, personal motives, and academic specialties.

In the field of Egyptology, the consensus of the profession ultimately colors everything, while facts presumably provide the building blocks of the foundation for any reasonable interpretation. In cases where evidence is slim, the trick can often be to find ways to "anchor" an interpretation by linking it to some immutable fact. In *The Great Pyramid Hoax,* Scott Creighton investigates various avenues for doing precisely that. He explores this anchoring principle as it applies to the evidence that supports the traditional dating of the Great Pyramid and to various theories that have been put forth over the years to question it. He takes consistent care to trace the evidence back to its earliest known sources and to consider many sides of a pertinent question. He is concerned about verifying the historical reasonableness of evidence; for example, does an inscription conform to the stylistic conventions of its attributed era, and was a specific formulation of paint available at the time when it is claimed to have been applied?

It is no wonder, in a field where competing viewpoints already struggle to take root within a broad set of informed academic researchers, that what may be perceived by those researchers as the less-well-informed viewpoints of outsiders are often not welcomed with open arms. Nonetheless, one proper role of the alternative researcher is to consider questions that may not be seen as politically correct within the more staid corridors of the traditional archaeologist. For myself, I was taught that it was the job of a scientist to dispassionately consider each of the potential answers to an important unresolved question, even those that might be considered unlikely or unpopular. Likewise, when it comes to issues that might theoretically fall through the cracks of peer review in a discipline as traditionally fraternal as Egyptology, there may still be value in subjecting important issues to the careful review of an outsider—one whose distance from the profession or differences in perspective may catalyze fresh new questions on a hotly debated subject.

Scott Creighton gives us this fresh perspective and so much more in *The Great Pyramid Hoax*.

LAIRD SCRANTON

LAIRD SCRANTON is a recognized authority on Dogon mythology and symbolism. He is a frequent guest on radio programs such as *Coast to Coast AM* and *Red Ice Radio* and has been a featured speaker on ancient mysteries at national conferences, including the Paradigm Symposium. He is the author of several books, including *The Science of the Dogon* and *China's Cosmological Prehistory*.

ACKNOWLEDGMENTS

This book would not have been possible without the input, assistance, and encouragement of many individuals. I would first like to express my profound and sincere gratitude to the team at Inner Traditions • Bear & Company, whose professionalism and guidance took much of the pain out of producing this work.

The late Zecharia Sitchin, a world-renowned scholar and international bestselling author, paved the way for this book, and without his early insights into this controversy, this work most likely would never have seen the light of day. This can be said equally of the late Alan F. Alford, whose dedicated research into this subject inspired much of my own investigations. In 1998, Alford wrote:

> My challenge to Egyptologists is this. Find the Howard Vyse diaries and show them to me. If I cannot find at least three incriminating statements in those diaries, I will drop my argument that the work-men's graffiti was forged.

It is with a considerable sense of regret that Alford, who departed this Earth much too soon, could not witness just how prophetic his words were to become as the evidence from three pages of Vyse's private diary, presented later in this book, will demonstrate.

Patricia Usick of the British Museum and Roger Bettridge of the Centre for Buckinghamshire Studies helped immensely by providing access to the Hill facsimiles and the Vyse family archive, respectively. I would particularly like to thank Mr. Bettridge for his great generosity in assisting me with the transcription of some difficult passages from Colonel Vyse's private journal. A special mention and thanks must also be extended to the staff in the Archive Department of the Mitchell Library in Glasgow, who also helped transcribe some difficult passages.

My good friend Sean Damer deserves credit here too for his unstinting support and encouragement over many years. And none of this would have been at all possible without the great help and assistance of George and Jim, who would tirelessly read and offer feedback to each draft of this manuscript.

My children, Jamie and Nina, were both very young when all of this began. They would always listen (sometimes reluctantly it has to be said), but they were always curious and would often ask questions. I thank them both for some quite marvelous questions; questions that only a child can ask.

Above all, my dearest wife, Louise, deserves all the plaudits for she has truly had to put up with the most—and it wasn't always plain sailing. When things got tough she was always there to help. And when they got really tough she was always the first with her shoulder to the wheel. Not even a severe head injury, which so nearly took her life, would hold her back. There are no words that can ever encapsulate my sincere gratitude in having this truly remarkable woman in my life.

I thank you all.

SCOTT CREIGHTON,
MIDSUMMER'S DAY, 2016

Louise Creighton
(Photo: Scott Creighton)

Introduction
A CONTROVERSIAL CLAIM

What is the truth of the crudely painted marks within four hidden chambers of the Great Pyramid of Giza, which were presented to the world by the British explorer and antiquarian Colonel Richard William Howard Vyse after blasting his way with gunpowder into these chambers in 1837?

To historians, archaeologists, and Egyptologists, these marks present hard evidence—the *only* hard evidence—that the Great Pyramid belonged to the ancient Egyptian king Khufu, who ruled Egypt circa 2550 BCE, and that it was probably built as his eternal tomb. According to the traditional view, the discovery of these painted marks gave to the world confirmation of the writings of the Greek historian Herodotus, who, some two thousand years *after* the Great Pyramid is believed to have been built, wrote that the structure had been erected as the eternal tomb of Cheops (the Greek word for Khufu), although the later historian Josephus (following Manetho) recorded the builder of the structure as Suphis, or Sensuphis, a name that linguists were eventually able to transliterate into its ancient Egyptian form of Khnum-Khuf and its abbreviated form, Khufu.

These roughly painted marks, which included three different names of the king (an ancient Egyptian king could have as many as *five* different names), are—without doubt—the strongest evidence that Egyptology has to link the Great Pyramid directly to Suphis/Khufu and thus to firmly lock the pyramid's construction to the date of circa 2550 BCE.

To an ever-increasing number of alternative thinkers, the site at

Giza, including the Sphinx and the Giza pyramids, is much, much older, and these painted marks allegedly discovered in situ are regarded as nothing more than the result of a quite audacious hoax perpetrated by Vyse and his team in order to confirm Suphis/Khufu as the builder of the Great Pyramid and thereby to provide corroboration to the ancient historical accounts of Herodotus, Manetho, and others that the Great Pyramid was built as the eternal tomb of this ancient Egyptian king.

In 1980, Russian-born, international bestselling author Zecharia Sitchin challenged the Egyptological establishment by publishing in his book *The Stairway to Heaven* a controversial claim that the painted marks, including the various king's names, deemed to have been discovered in the Great Pyramid by Vyse were, in fact, forged by him. While Sitchin raised some pertinent questions concerning Vyse's claimed discovery— some of which remain legitimate questions even to this day—the main evidence he presented in support of his forgery theory was eventually discredited. As a result, Sitchin's controversial allegation was soon dismissed, and many of those who had hitherto supported him quickly distanced themselves from the controversy.

Now, almost forty years after Sitchin first made his forgery allegation, *The Great Pyramid Hoax* revisits this highly controversial question and presents a dossier of new and never-before-seen evidence that strongly suggests that Sitchin's forgery claim (while largely unsupported by the evidence Sitchin himself presented) may, in fact, have been right all along, and that, far from being the near impossible task that mainstream Egyptology claims it would have been, such a forgery could have been carried out by Vyse with just the most elementary knowledge of the ancient Egyptian language—and a little bit of luck.

The evidence presented in this book comes from a variety of sources, old and new: from Vyse's little-known private field notes as well as his published work, from the survey and facsimile drawings made at the time by his assistants, and from modern high-definition photographs, eyewitness accounts, modern chemical analysis, and other credible sources.

With all of these sources at our disposal we find ourselves, like the best historical detectives, prying open this "cold case" as we comb the byways and alleyways of recent and ancient history, compiling a compelling dossier of highly incriminating facts that strongly suggests that the painted "quarry marks" in these chambers—in particular the various royal names of the king—were almost certainly faked by Vyse and his team.

To many of us today, the implication of such a hoax having been perpetrated within the Great Pyramid is—quite literally—monumental, for, at a stroke, the Great Pyramid is removed almost entirely from the historical context into which conventional Egyptology has effectively shoehorned the structure. But if the evidence of the crudely painted marks found within the pyramid truly was faked, then, at a stroke, Egyptology loses the key piece of evidence that allows it to attribute the structure to Khufu and to a construction date of circa 2550 BCE. With this vital evidence removed, then the Giza pyramids become monuments whose provenance is much less certain and, as such, reopens the question as to who really was the builder of these monuments, when were they built, and for what purpose.

This is *The Great Pyramid Hoax.*

1
MAKING HISTORY

The Great Pyramid of Giza in Egypt is said by historians to have been the tomb of Khufu (the Greek Suphis, or Cheops), an ancient Egyptian king who ruled the land of the Nile some 4,500 years ago and who is believed to have been the second king of the Fourth Dynasty of the ancient Egyptian civilization.

Alas, however, neither the remains of Khufu nor any of his funerary equipment were ever found within the Great Pyramid, the structure supposedly having been pillaged and picked clean in antiquity by tomb robbers, according to the traditional narrative. Indeed, the only direct physical evidence Egyptology has to connect the Great Pyramid of Giza to this Fourth Dynasty king are some rough, red-painted marks that are claimed to have been discovered by British explorer and antiquarian Colonel Richard William Howard Vyse (fig. 1.1), who claims he

Fig. 1.1. Colonel Richard William Howard Vyse

4

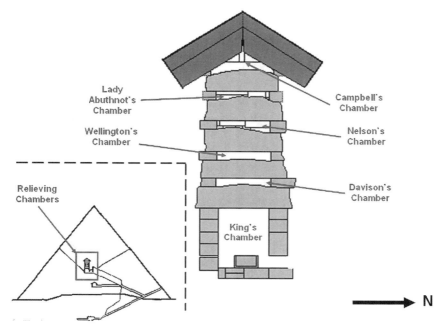

Fig. 1.2. The five "stress relieving chambers" of the Great Pyramid.
The upper four chambers were blasted open by Vyse in 1837.
(Image: Scott Creighton)

found the marks inscribed on the stone walls and roof of a series of hidden "stress relieving chambers" that had been sealed since the pyramid's construction (fig. 1.2).

Among the profusion of marks found on the stone blocks of these small chambers were some highly significant inscriptions that, according to Egyptologists, present the various names of the king they believe built the Great Pyramid.

It has come down to us via the fragmented accounts of the ancient historians Herodotus, Manetho, and some others that the builder of the Great Pyramid was known in ancient times as Cheops (according to Herodotus) and Suphis (according to Manetho). Historians accept that these two Greek names refer to the same historical person—the man they believe constructed the Great Pyramid. After Jean-François Champollion—building on the earlier efforts of Sir Thomas Young—

Fig. 1.3. Egyptian hieroglyphs spelling Khnum-Khuf—the full birth name of Khufu. Note how this name is contained within an oval frame known as a cartouche.

Fig. 1.4. Egyptian hieroglyphs spelling Khufu. The vertical bar (at the left of the cartouche) always indicates the end of the name.

finally succeeded in cracking the ancient Egyptian hieroglyphic system in 1822, the name Cheops/Suphis was, ten years later in 1832, transliterated by the pioneering Italian Egyptologist Ippolito Rosellini into the hieroglyphic form of the name Khnum-Khuf and its abbreviated form, Khufu (figs. 1.3 and 1.4).

As stated, both Khnum-Khuf and its abbreviated form, Khufu, are said to have been found in a number of hidden chambers of the Great Pyramid. However, these marks were not neatly sculpted hieroglyphic signs like those in figures 1.3 and 1.4 but instead were simple, crudely painted hieroglyphic signs written in a cursive style known by scholars today as *old hieratic,* a shorthand script used for everyday communication (figs. 1.5 and 1.6). The red ochre paint used to make these marks was made from iron oxide ochre mixed into water, sometimes with fish oil, gum, egg, or honey added to act as a binding agent. This simple paint, known as *moghra,* was still being made and was still available in Egypt in 1837.

Fig. 1.5. Reproduction of Egyptian cursive script (old hieratic) spelling Khnum-Khuf (Image: Scott Creighton, based on original drawing by J. S. Perring)

Fig. 1.6. Reproduction of Egyptian cursive script (old hieratic) spelling Khufu (Image: Scott Creighton, based on original drawing by J. R. Hill)

The signs used in old hieratic script were cursively painted equivalents of the sculpted hieroglyphs, and, as such, their early orthography was not so far removed from their counterpart sculpted signs. As the centuries passed, however, the ink or painted cursive signs became ever more simplified (for ease of writing), resulting in the hieratic signs becoming ever more cursive, evolving further and further away from the sculpted hieroglyphic form from which many (though not all) of the hieratic signs originated. In later dynasties the written hieratic signs had evolved to the point of bearing no likeness whatsoever to their root sculpted hieroglyphic equivalents. This was called *demotic script.* By contrast, many of the sculpted, or "monumental," hieroglyphic signs changed very little over the entire duration of the ancient Egyptian civilization.

In short, old hieratic signs, whether written neatly with ink and reed on a sheet of papyrus or crudely written with paint and brush on a block of stone, were obviously much quicker forms of writing than the labor-intensive sculpted stone hieroglyphics, and, as a consequence, the signs naturally became much more cursive and simplified in appearance than the traditional monumental form (figs. 1.5 and 1.6).

As the study of ancient Egyptian hieroglyphics progressed and the names of the various kings became ever more understood, it was realized that not only did these hidden chambers discovered by Vyse contain the full and abbreviated birth name of the king but that a *third* name of the Great Pyramid builder had also been inscribed onto the walls of these hidden chambers. This other name became known as the king's Horus name (fig. 1.7), and, significantly, this name was *not* contained within the distinctive oval cartouche, which, in Vyse's time, was understood as the only means by which the king's name could be recognized.

As stated in the introduction to this book, it is now understood that an ancient Egyptian king could have as many as five different names, although, it has to be said, this was *not* fully understood in Vyse's time. And so, with all of these different royal names of the Great Pyramid builder painted onto a number of stone blocks of the various relief chambers, Egyptologists now had more than the mere word of Herodotus and Manetho to support their view that Suphis/Khnum-Khuf (a.k.a. Khufu/Medjedu) built the Great Pyramid.

But there is much more to Vyse's claimed discovery. These inscriptions within the Great Pyramid were not simple isolated inscriptions of the king's various names, but were, in fact, contained within phrases consisting of a series of other signs alongside (or below) the king's name. It is now believed that these other signs (along with the king's name) formed the identities of the various work gangs (figs. 1.8–1.10) involved

Fig. 1.7. Reproduction of Egyptian cursive script spelling Hor Medjedu (Khufu's Horus name). Note that the Horus name is not contained within the distinctive oval cartouche. (Image: Scott Creighton, based on original drawing by J. R. Hill)

Fig. 1.8. Reproduction of a gang name from the Great Pyramid that reads, "The gang, the White Crown of Khnum-Khuf is powerful." Note: actual orientation of script maintained. (Image: Scott Creighton, based on original drawing by J. R. Hill)

Fig. 1.9. Reproduction of a gang name from the Great Pyramid that reads, "The gang, Companions of Khufu." Note: actual orientation of script maintained. (Image: Scott Creighton, based on original drawing by J. R. Hill)

Fig. 1.10. Reproduction of a gang name from the Great Pyramid that reads, "The gang, Pure Ones of the Hor Medjedu." (Image: Scott Creighton, based on original drawing by J. S. Perring)

in constructing the pyramid, and it is believed that these names were painted onto individual stone blocks by the various quarry gangs as they extracted the blocks at the stone quarries, which is why these writings are called quarry marks or workers' graffiti. Within the hidden chambers three different quarry gang names were found, although the precise translations of these names remain somewhat uncertain.

And so, with this highly compelling material, Egyptology felt supremely confident that it now had sufficient authentic documentary evidence to declare Suphis/Khufu as the builder of the Great Pyramid.

AN IMPOSSIBLE FORGERY

But there were other reasons why Egyptologists could feel confident that the painted marks in these chambers were authentic Old Kingdom marks and not, as a number of researchers have suggested—most notably Zecharia Sitchin (fig. 1.11)—fake marks painted onto the chamber walls by Vyse and his team.

These reasons can be summarized as follows:

1. Both the full birth name of the king (Khnum-Khuf) and its abbreviated form (Khufu) as well as the Horus name appear in these hidden chambers of the Great Pyramid. There are six, mostly complete, occurrences of Khnum-Khuf (fig. 1.5), one complete occurrence of Khufu (fig. 1.6), and four occurrences of Hor Medjedu (fig. 1.7) to be observed within the various chambers. However, in 1837 no one anywhere in the world knew that an ancient Egyptian king could shorten his birth name or, as noted, that the king could have as many as five different royal names. So, the reasoning goes, if these marks had been faked, why would any forger have placed what would have appeared to the forger to be *two* different (though similar) royal cartouches within these chambers if, as it was understood in 1837, the pyramid was built as the eternal tomb of just *one* king? Why not place *only* the Khnum-Khuf cartouche name or *only* the Khufu cartouche name within these chambers? In short, why would

Fig. 1.11. Zecharia Sitchin (1920–2010) first suggested the painted marks within the hidden chambers of the Great Pyramid were faked by Vyse.

any hoaxer at this time have placed *two* cartouches into the chambers when it would surely have been known to the hoaxer that the Great Pyramid was built by one king, known as Suphis?

2. No one in 1837 knew that the king had another royal name known as the Horus name, which was *not* written within the distinctive royal cartouche. As noted, it was believed in Vyse's time that the names of ancient Egyptian kings were always written inside an oval cartouche. How then, the Egyptologists argue, would it have been possible for any forger to recognize a piece of ancient Egyptian script as another name for the king (i.e., the Horus name) and place it also within these chambers when this name wasn't even inside a cartouche, the distinguishing oval sign that would have easily identified the text therein as a king's name? For someone to possess such knowledge, the Egyptologists insist, would have made that individual the foremost scholar and authority of ancient Egyptian writing in the world. In 1837 such knowledge would have been beyond even the best academic minds of the time and would, they insist, have been far beyond the reach of the average forger—so it is believed.

3. Some of the quarry marks can only be observed through small cracks between tightly fitting adjacent blocks. How would it have been possible, the Egyptologists ask, for any forger to get a brush into the tight gaps between these immovable, seventy-ton blocks and paint any meaningful marks onto the faces of those closely fitting blocks? These marks, they insist, had to have been painted onto the blocks *before* they were set into place (i.e., when the block faces were accessible at the quarries), so they conclude that *all* the painted marks, including those in plain sight, *must* be genuine.

4. It is argued also by Egyptologists that each of the work gangs that built the pyramid (and its internal chambers) had quite different names and that each individual gang name was only ever linked to a specific version of the king's five names; these gang names were quite specific and were never mixed and matched. How could any forger possibly have known of this "pairing" of a specific gang name to a specific version of the king's name?

5. Related to point 4 above is the theory proposed by Egyptologists that each work gang was responsible for the construction of a particular side of the pyramid (and, presumably, the same side of the internal chambers). To this end it is argued that the work gangs responsible for particular sides of the pyramid (and its internal chambers) would place their names *only* on the blocks for the side of the pyramid or the pyramid chamber that they were responsible for constructing. How could any forger have possibly known of such a practice and (according to Egyptologist Ann Macy Roth, Ph.D.) have then replicated such a practice onto the stones within the various stress-relieving chambers of the Great Pyramid?*

---

*There are five so-called relieving chambers built above the King's Chamber in the Great Pyramid. Some Egyptologists believe they were built to relieve the tremendous weight of the pyramid structure that is pressing down on the King's Chamber. To do this, massive granite and limestone blocks were stacked to form open spaces (i.e., chambers) above the roof of the King's Chamber, thereby deflecting some of the weight off the King's Chamber. The puzzle remains, though, as to why no such measures were taken for the Queen's Chamber, which has even more weight bearing down on it.

6. During a visit to these hidden chambers of the Great Pyramid, geologist and geophysicist Robert M. Schoch, Ph.D., visually examined many of the painted marks therein, and what he found convinced him of their authenticity, writing, "Were these just fakes? Studying them closely, however, they looked authentically ancient to me. I could see later mineral crystals precipitated over them . . ."[1]

Together, all of the above points represent a summary of the key facts that mainstream Egyptologists present in support of their view that the painted marks in the Great Pyramid are genuine Old Kingdom quarry marks and are not and could never have been the product of a nineteenth-century hoax, as first proposed by Zecharia Sitchin in his controversial book *The Stairway to Heaven*. As such, Egyptology insists that there is little need for any modern scientific analysis, or further research of any kind, into the question of the authenticity and provenance of these marks. In their view a forgery would have been impossible; thus, the quarry marks are genuine, and that is the end of the matter.

SITCHIN'S FORGERY CLAIM

In his book Sitchin argued that Vyse and his assistant, J. R. Hill (with the tacit complicity of another assistant, John Shea Perring), painted the Khnum-Khuf and Khufu cartouches into the various chambers of the Great Pyramid. He writes:

His depiction thus served to enhance Vyse's and Hill's notion that the crucial cartouche of Kh-u-f-u should be inscribed in the uppermost chamber with the symbol for the solar disk. . . . But in doing so, the inscriber had employed the hieroglyphic symbol and phonetic sound for RA, the supreme god of Egypt! He had unwittingly spelled out not Khnem-Khuf, but Khnem-Rauf; not Khufu but Raufu. He had used the name of the great god incorrectly and in vain; it was blasphemy in ancient Egypt. . . .

And, therefore, the substitution of Ra for Kh was an error that could not have been committed in the time of Khufu, nor of any ancient Pharaoh. Only a stranger to hieroglyphics, a stranger to Khufu, and a stranger to the overpowering worship of Ra, could have committed such a grave error.[2]

In his later book *Journeys to the Mythical Past,* Sitchin expanded on his forgery theory, writing:

As I was poring over Vyse's printed diary [Vyse's published work], something odd struck me: The Royal name he showed was inscribed differently than on the Inventory Stela; instead of diagonal lines (a "sieve") inside a circle which reads KH (and thus KH-U-F-U), Vyse's finds were written with a circle with just a dot inside . . . that reads not KH but RA, the sacred name of Egypt's supreme god. Thus the name Vyse reported was not Khufu but RA-u-f-u.

In 1978, visiting the British Museum, I asked to see the Vyse parchments. It took some doing, as no one had asked for them as far as anyone could recall. But the Hill Facsimiles (as they were catalogued) were found and shown to me—a bundle tied with yellowing-white ribbon. The authenticated parchments were there, the way they reached the museum more than a century earlier; and the misspelling was also there: In no instance was the "Kh" inscribed correctly as a sieve with diagonal lines; instead there was a dot or a smudge inside a circle, spelling "Ra."[3]

It is difficult to know where to begin with Sitchin's comments on this issue. The first thing to say is that Sitchin was relying on the survey drawings made by Perring that were included in Vyse's published work. However, these plan drawings of the chambers present the chamber markings and the various cartouches therein in much too small a scale to be able to easily or clearly discern the fine detail within the cartouche discs.

Second, despite an attempt to do so, Sitchin never managed to obtain a permit that would have allowed him access to the relieving chambers of the Great Pyramid to witness the cartouches therein firsthand. Had he managed to do this then he would have realized the complete folly of his own words. Photographs and epigraphic drawings of the Khufu cartouche from Campbell's Chamber (a cartouche on which Sitchin focused his argument) clearly show that this cartouche does indeed contain very obvious horizontal striations and *not* a center smudge or dot, as Sitchin claimed in his books.

Even more bizarre is Sitchin's claim that the facsimile drawings of Hill (now in the British Museum) do not contain the "correct" striations. Having seen all twenty-eight of Hill's facsimiles and compared them with Perring's survey drawings, I can vouch that they do, in fact, show that all the cartouche discs match. The cartouche disc lines in Hill's facsimile drawings are horizontal, as are those in Perring's drawings. (Unfortunately there are, at present, no publicly available photographs of the Khnum-Khuf cartouches from the relieving chambers of the Great Pyramid that would allow us better comparisons.) Why Sitchin seemed to think the disc striations of the cartouches within these chambers could only be diagonal is unclear as it was known in Sitchin's time that these lines within the cartouche disc can be diagonal, horizontal, or even vertical, and there seems to be no rule that stipulates how many lines should be drawn within the disc; there can be many, and, significantly, there can even be *no* striations present, a point we will come back to later in this book.

But most pertinent here is that the facsimile drawing of the Khufu cartouche made by Hill from Campbell's Chamber most certainly agrees with photographic evidence of the actual cartouche in this chamber that we observe today—a disc with three clear horizontal striations and not a dot or a smudge. It has to be said though that there is a single occurrence of a cartouche drawing made by Hill from one of the lower chambers whereby the lines within the cartouche disc are so close together that they do appear as a single smudge that could be taken as a center dot. If this single instance of a cartouche disc that *looks* like it has a center dot is what Sitchin based his Ra argument on, then Sitchin is surely guilty of being highly selective with his evidence while, at the same time, ignoring the large body of evidence (facsimile drawings) that contradicted his argument.

It is simply difficult to fathom what Sitchin was trying to say about

Hill's drawings, particularly the facsimile of the Khufu cartouche in Campbell's Chamber, for this cartouche (at least the publicly available photographs of it) totally agrees with what I found myself in Hill's drawings of it at the British Museum. (There are, however, some other, newly discovered anomalies with Hill's drawing of this gang name and its associated Khufu cartouche, which will be discussed in chapter 11.)

When the flaws in Sitchin's forgery claim were exposed, it is understandable that other renowned and respected authors such as Graham Hancock and Robert Bauval, who had hitherto backed Sitchin's forgery claim in their own books, quickly distanced themselves from the controversy. Through his failure to properly research these chamber cartouches (at the very least obtain photographic evidence of the actual Khufu cartouche from Campbell's Chamber), Sitchin's flawed research has served only to "poison the well," making it very difficult indeed for other researchers to revisit the forgery question. Most people now consider that, with Sitchin's key argument having been debunked, the matter is now settled and closed.

So, as a result of the flawed aspects of Sitchin's research having rightly been dismissed, Vyse's history-making discovery of these painted marks that bear the various names of the second king of the Fourth Dynasty of ancient Egypt has continued to go unchallenged and, to this day, remains the key piece of tangible evidence that links the Great Pyramid to Suphis/Khufu/Hor Medjedu. With Vyse's unchallenged evidence, the Great Pyramid was duly slotted by Egyptology into the epoch of circa 2550 BCE—making it a structure that now firmly belonged to the Old Kingdom period of ancient Egypt.

On the surface the painted quarry marks in the relieving chambers seem highly compelling evidence, and there would appear to be little reason why anyone should ever begin to doubt or even question their authenticity or provenance, and the case for the Egyptologists is now surely beyond question.

But is it? Is the mainstream case really so watertight, so impregnable? What we must keep in mind here is that these painted marks have never, as far as we are presently aware, been subjected to any official, modern scientific scrutiny; their authenticity was accepted by

Egyptology purely on what amounts to little more than the word of Vyse and bolstered by the belief that any forgery would have been virtually impossible, especially by someone such as Vyse, who had a very limited understanding of ancient Egyptian hieroglyphics. Such was the standard of proof of these things in early Victorian Britain.

But was it really so impossible for someone at that time with very limited knowledge of ancient Egyptian language and writing to have confounded all of the perceived obstacles and to somehow have managed to find a way to convincingly and successfully forge these painted marks? Was there any possibility at all that any layperson in Vyse's time could have placed these marks into these chambers, even in impossible places between tight-fitting blocks, in a manner that is consistent with our modern understanding of them, to have fooled the experts of the time and thus to have effectively perpetrated the hoax of all history?

Sitchin's flawed research notwithstanding, in consideration of this question, it is the opinion of this author that the answer has to be an emphatic "yes"; it was entirely possible for someone in 1837, with just the most elementary knowledge of ancient Egyptian hieroglyphics and just a sprinkling of luck, to have pulled off such an audacious hoax and to have done so in a manner that was convincing and not at odds with the contemporary understanding of the marks. Consider the following:

1. Contrary to the view of Egyptology, to perpetrate such a hoax did not at all require any in-depth understanding of ancient Egyptian hieroglyphics or hieratic script in order to "know" what were "appropriate" marks to place inside these hidden chambers.
2. Any hoaxer would need only to have the ability to recognize the cartouche of Suphis/Khufu to perpetrate this hoax, and it will be shown that Vyse most certainly *was* able to recognize the Suphis/Khufu cartouche during his time in Egypt.
3. Acting on the state of scholarly knowledge of the time, any hoaxer would actually have been compelled to find and place not one but *two* (similar looking) cartouches into the various chambers.
4. Contrary to the view of Egyptology, painting marks into tight gaps between immovable blocks is actually quite feasible and not

the impossible task Egyptology would have us believe; it required only a little lateral thinking on the part of the hoaxer.

5. While it is unlikely that the practice of different ancient Egyptian crews working on different sides of the pyramid and on the sides of the internal chambers (as theorized by Ann Macy Roth) would have been known to any hoaxer, a close analysis of the distribution of the various marks in these chambers seems to suggest that, contrary to the view of Roth, whoever placed the marks in these chambers did *not*, in fact, adhere to or understand such a practice.

6. The visual observation of the painted marks by Schoch in which he described them as looking "authentically ancient" as a result of "later mineral crystals [having] precipitated over them" is inconclusive without actual chemical analysis of the marks (which will be presented later in this book). Further on in this passage, Schoch goes on to say of this mineral crystallization that it is ". . . a process that takes centuries or millennia" If the crystallization observed on these marks can, in Schoch's words, take just "centuries" to form, then they could just as easily have formed in the near two centuries since Vyse first opened these chambers (and thereby forever changing the atmospheric conditions within them). Indeed, photographs of some modern graffiti to the left of the Khufu cartouche shows this graffiti entirely clear of any crystallization but is almost entirely covered with crystals in more recent images—crystallization that has taken, at most, just a few decades to form.

In the course of this book we will consider in detail how all of these seemingly insurmountable obstacles could have been overcome by Vyse and his team (and relatively easily so), as well as present the considerable corpus of evidence that strongly suggests that the painted marks within these chambers are not the provenance of the Fourth Dynasty of ancient Egypt but are nothing more than the product of a nineteenth-century hoax. In short, the forthcoming chapters of this book will demonstrate how such a hoax *could* have been easily perpetrated and will present numerous evidence-based facts that show that, in all likelihood, such a hoax *was* perpetrated.

However, before we delve in to the details of this, it might stand us in good stead to present a quick-and-basic outline as to how such a hoax could have been perpetrated within the Great Pyramid.

CHAPTER ONE SUMMARY

- Vyse discovered and opened four chambers above the King's Chamber within the Great Pyramid. These chambers presented the first and only written text ever found in any of the giant pyramids. The text consisted of rough quarry marks painted onto the stone blocks of the chambers with red ochre paint, a paint that was still being made and available in Egypt in 1837.
- Among the marks found were the various names of Suphis, the ancient Egyptian king whom Egyptologists believe built the Great Pyramid. The king's names formed part of the names of the work gangs who built the pyramid.
- One of the names found was not even known, at this time, to be a king's name, as it was not contained within the distinctive royal cartouche that would normally characterize and identify the royal name.
- These painted marks provided Egyptologists with physical evidence connecting the pyramid to Suphis/Khufu and thus to the Fourth Dynasty of ancient Egypt circa 2550 BCE.
- Zecharia Sitchin, in his 1980 book, *The Stairway to Heaven,* claimed that these quarry marks were painted into the pyramid's upper chambers by Vyse and his closest assistants, who discovered and blasted their way into the chambers.
- Some of the evidence presented by Sitchin in support of his forgery claim was later found to be flawed, and, as such, his claim was dismissed, even though some of the other evidence he presented in support of his claim has never been properly addressed.
- It will be shown that it is perfectly feasible to place marks in small gaps between closely fitting blocks.

- Contrary to the mainstream belief that the state of hieroglyphic knowledge in 1837 would not have permitted Vyse or anyone else to have perpetrated such a hoax, it will be shown that such a hoax could easily have been perpetrated with just the most elementary knowledge of ancient Egyptian hieroglyphics.
- Schoch believes that quarry marks on the blocks are authentic ancient marks based on crystallization on the surface of some marks. He states also that this crystallization process can take millennia or just centuries to occur.

2
SEEKING SUPHIS

Prior to his claimed discovery of the Suphis/Khufu cartouche in the Great Pyramid, it is now known that Vyse clearly knew how this particular cartouche should be written. Evidence from his private journal, which will be presented in chapter 13, clearly demonstrates his foreknowledge of this cartouche during his time in Egypt. Curiously, this pivotal understanding is never revealed by Vyse in his *published* work, and it remains unclear exactly *how* Vyse managed to acquire this crucial knowledge as the study of Egyptian hieroglyphics was very much in its infancy, with very little having been published at this time.

It was well understood in Vyse's time (from the ancient historian Manetho) that the builder of the Great Pyramid was known as Suphis. However, in 1837, apart from a few academics, very few people in the world would have known which of the hundreds of ancient Egyptian kings' cartouches represented or could be transliterated into the Greek *Suphis*. This is to say that if anyone were to perpetrate a hoax inside the Great Pyramid, they would have had to ensure that whatever king's cartouche they selected to place inside the chambers, it would have to be a cartouche that transliterated into the Greek *Suphis*. A forger simply could not select a cartouche at random, place it into the pyramid, and hope it would be accepted by scholars as the correct cartouche.

Identifying the correct cartouche of Suphis was not an easy task by any means. The key knowledge in Vyse's time with regard to the translations of the cartouches of the ancient Egyptian kings lay in the hands of just a few scholars, such as the British academic

Sir John Gardner Wilkinson, the Italian Egyptologist Ippolito Rosellini, Samuel Birch of the British Museum, and also some keen amateurs such as Major Orlando Felix.

In *The Stairway to Heaven,* Sitchin writes the following about Wilkinson's 1828 book, *Materia Hieroglyphica.*

> The one and only book repeatedly mentioned in Vyse's chronicles is (Sir) John Gardner Wilkinson's *Materia Hieroglyphica.* As its title page declared, it aimed to update the reader on "the Egyptian Pantheon and the Succession of the Pharaohs from the earliest times to the conquest of Alexander." Published in 1828—nine years before Vyse's assault on the pyramids—it was a standard book for English Egyptologists.
>
> Birch had stated in his report, "a cartouche, similar to that which first occurs in Wellington's Chamber, had been published by Mr. Wilkinson *Mater. Hieroglyph.*" We thus have a clear indication of the probable source of the cartouche inscribed by Hill in the very first chamber (Wellington's) found by Vyse.[1]

Wilkinson's *Materia Hieroglyphica* was indeed one of the earliest published works (in English) relating to the study and understanding of ancient Egyptian hieroglyphics. However, a perusal of Wilkinson's book shows that, contrary to Sitchin's comments (based on the comments of Birch), there is no cartouche of Khnum-Khuf or of Khufu in this early work of Wilkinson. Birch's comment suggesting the Khnum-Khuf cartouche was identified and published in *Materia Hieroglyphica* is erroneous,[2] and it may be that Birch intended to cite Wilkinson's later work, *Manners and Customs of the Ancient Egyptians* (1837), which does indeed present the Khnum-Khuf cartouche and its abbreviated Khufu form, as well as identifying these cartouches as spelling the names of Sensuphis and Suphis, respectively. However, it would have been quite unlikely that Vyse could have procured any helpful knowledge from this later work by Wilkinson, because it was not generally available until January 1838, by which time Vyse had already completed his operations at Giza and had returned to England.

Another possible source that might have assisted any potential forger was the list of kings presented by Felix in his *Notes on Hieroglyphics* (1830). In Felix's list of "Uncertain Kings" from Wadi Maghara (fig. 2.1) we find the cartouche of Khnum-Khuf and also the cartouche for its abbreviated form, Khufu. Significantly though, Felix does not identify either of these cartouches with the name Suphis, so we must also dismiss this work as providing any useful information that might have assisted any potential hoaxer. The best that could be hoped for with Felix's list of "Uncertain Kings" is that it considerably reduced the number of possible candidates for the all-important Suphis cartouche.

Two years later, in 1832, Rosellini published his *I'Monumenti Dell'Egitto e Della Nubia*. In this scholarly tome we find, for the first time, the cartouches of Khnum-Khuf and Khufu published and identified with the names of Suphis (Khufu) and Sensuphis (Khnum-Khuf) (fig. 2.2).

Fig. 2.1. Example of Major Felix's "Uncertain Kings" from Wadi Maghara, showing the cartouches of Khnum-Khuf and Khufu (Image: Major Orlando Felix)

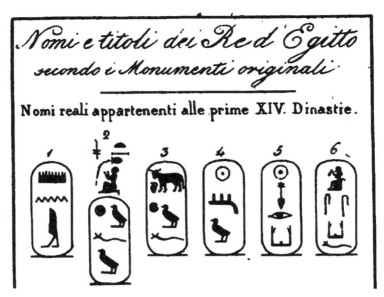

*Fig. 2.2. The Suphis/Khufu cartouche (#2) and the
Sensuphis/Khnum-Khuf (#3) are identified by Rosellini.
(Image: Ippolito Rosellini)*

So here in Rosellini's work of 1832, some four years *before* Vyse had
embarked upon his operations in Egypt, we find both of the cartouches
found in the various relieving chambers of the Great Pyramid identified
with the names of Suphis and Sensuphis, and, as such, Rosellini's book
would most certainly have assisted any potential forger, providing as it
does, the key cartouche identified as "Suphis."

But Vyse would have needed more than just the correct cartouche
to convincingly pull off such a hoax. In this regard it is proposed that
Vyse, and/or his assistants, discovered a cache of authentic, old hieratic texts (perhaps painted onto stone or written with ink on papyrus)
somewhere *outside* the Great Pyramid (as originally proposed by the
author and alternative historian Alan Alford); Old Kingdom hieratic
inscriptions that would have included various gang names of which the
Khnum-Khuf and Khufu cartouches form a part. This "secret cache"
would also have contained other inscriptions, including Khufu's Horus
name, Hor Medjedu.

However, even though he would not have been able to comprehend anything other than the two cartouches in this theorized secret cache, Vyse would have logically deduced that *all* of the markings presented therein were clearly related in some way to Suphis/Khufu (by virtue of having been found along with the Suphis/Khufu cartouche—the one inscription Vyse *could* recognize). These additional markings, even although incomprehensible to Vyse, would have been copied into the various chambers. In this scenario Vyse requires only the ability to recognize the cartouche of Suphis/Khufu—this is his "primer," his "cue." Most of the other inscriptions, including the cartouche-less Horus name, placed by Vyse and his team into these chambers merely follow on from this basic, but crucial, piece of knowledge.

Because both the Khufu and Khnum-Khuf cartouches are quite similar, it is further proposed that Vyse assumed the Khnum-Khuf cartouche was simply a variation of the Khufu cartouche but that they both essentially represented the *same* king. Vyse could conceivably have come to such a conclusion had he studied Wilkinson's *Materia Hieroglyphica* in which the eminent British scholar writes:

1. That the phonetic names are always contained in the oval . . . which I shall distinguish by the word "nomen."

2. That the other oval, or prenomen, always contains a *title,* derived from the name of one, or more deities, which serves to point out more particularly the king, to whom both the ovals belong.[3]

In reading the above passage in Wilkinson's book, it is perfectly conceivable that Vyse could have concluded (erroneously) that the two slightly different ovals (cartouches) of Khufu and Khnum-Khuf he had found (in the proposed secret cache) were but the nomen and prenomen names of the same king (rather than one cartouche actually being but an abbreviated form of the other, which is the present belief of Egyptologists). This erroneous assumption of Vyse (in reading Wilkinson) would have effectively ensured that he would have *both* cartouches (from the secret cache) placed within the various chambers of the Great Pyramid. Furthermore, Vyse would not have known that one of the incomprehensible inscriptions from his secret cache that he would also have copied into the chambers was actually *another* of the king's names, the Horus name (Hor Medjedu), a name (not placed in the distinctive cartouche) that would only be identified as a royal name long after his operations in 1837.

To continue the forgery hypothesis, it is further proposed that

1. Some of the markings in these hidden chambers of the Great Pyramid are, in fact, genuine. There is good evidence to support this.

2. The Khnum-Khuf cartouche discovered by Vyse would have contained a disc with internal horizontal striations, whereas the Khufu cartouche would have initially contained a disc with *no* internal striations—just a blank disc.

3. The Khufu cartouche from the proposed secret cache would have been found also with two small dots beneath the snake glyph.

4. The markings (from Vyse's proposed secret cache) would have been painted into the various chambers by two of Vyse's assistants, Raven and Hill, shortly after the chambers were blasted open with gunpowder.

5. Shortly after placing the Khufu cartouche (initially with a blank disc) on the gabled roof of Campbell's Chamber, Vyse would have learned of another spelling for the disc in this cartouche, a spelling that presented this cartouche disc not as blank but with three internal, horizontal striations. These striations would have been added a few weeks later to the (previously copied) blank cartouche disc in Campbell's Chamber and certainly before Hill sent his (updated) facsimile drawing of this cartouche to London.

While the above represents a brief hypothesis of how a forgery could have been perpetrated in the Great Pyramid in 1837, just how likely is it that Vyse would have actually carried out such a fraud? Was he the type of man who could and would have carried out such an audacious hoax, and, if so, what might his motivation have been for so doing? In order to try and answer these questions it may help us to consider the type of man Vyse was and to understand a little of his background.

CHAPTER TWO SUMMARY

- From a study of his private field notes, it is quite clear that Vyse was familiar with the Suphis/Khufu cartouche and how it should be written. It remains unclear how Vyse obtained this crucial knowledge.
- Sir John Gardner Wilkinson's *Materia Hieroglyphica* (1828) did not identify the Suphis cartouche. While Wilkinson's *Manner and Customs of the Ancient Egyptians* (1837) did correctly identify the Suphis cartouche, it was published too late for it to have assisted Vyse, who had, by the time of that book's publication, already completed his operations at Giza and returned to England.
- Wilkinson's *Materia Hieroglyphica,* along with his later work *Topography of Thebes and General View of Egypt* (1835), could have given Vyse the information that an ancient Egyptian king would have had two names, a nomen and prenomen, and that these two names could appear quite similar. Vyse may have mistaken the Khnum-Khuf and Khufu cartouches as a nomen and prenomen of the same king, even though Khufu is actually just an abbreviated form of the nomen Khnum-Khuf. Wilkinson's 1835 book was found in Vyse's private library after his death in 1855.
- Major Orlando Felix's *Notes on Hieroglyphics* (1830) presented the two cartouches found within the Great Pyramid but did not identify them as Suphis/Sensuphis.
- Ippolito Rosellini's *I'Monumenti Dell'Egitto e Della Nubia* (1832) presented the two cartouches found within the Great Pyramid and identified them as Suphis and Sensuphis. This was published five years or so before Vyse commenced his operations at Giza.
- It is proposed that Vyse discovered a secret cache of authentic old hieratic script somewhere outside the pyramid. This proposed secret

cache would have consisted mainly of the gang names of the pyramid builders, of which the king's name forms a part of the gang name. Other hieratic marks would also have been found. All of these marks, with the exception of the cartouches, would likely have been unintelligible to Vyse. But because they were found together, they were all clearly related. As such they could all be safely copied as work gang graffiti into the Great Pyramid at suitable locations.

• The Suphis/Khufu cartouche, which Vyse could have recognized as a king's name, is the only cue that he would have needed to successfully pull off a convincing hoax.

• Acting on information received from Perring, Vyse could have later learned that the disc within the Khufu cartouche he had copied (from his secret cache) into Campbell's Chamber could have different spellings. Realizing he had copied what he now believed to be an incorrect spelling of the disc into the chamber, he would subsequently have the cartouche disc slightly altered to reflect what he now believed was the correct spelling. Hill would also update his facsimile drawing of the cartouche disc with this new information before sending it to the British Museum in London.

• Some genuine red ochre paint markings would be found within some of these hidden chambers.

3

MAN OF MEANS

It would be easy to characterize Vyse (fig. 3.1) in a particular light, as a one-dimensional, cardboard-cutout villain who took advantage of and exploited a situation for his own ends—for fame if not for fortune. But, as with everyone, the man was a much more complex character.

Born Richard William Vyse on July 25, 1784, he was the only son of General Richard Vyse of Standon, Comptroller of the Household of H.R.H. the Duke of Cumberland, and his wife, Lady Ann Howard (a descendant of the Howards of Norfolk), the daughter and heiress of Field Marshal Sir George Howard. In 1812, by royal sign-manual, young Vyse took on the additional name of Howard (from his mother), which

Fig. 3.1. Self-portrait of Colonel Richard William Howard Vyse, painted in 1816 (Photo: Leonard Cottrell, The Mountains of Pharaoh, *Robert Hale Ltd.)*

Fig. 3.2. Stoke Place, Colonel Richard William Howard Vyse's country estate, Buckinghamshire, England

allowed him to inherit from his maternal grandmother, Lucy, daughter of Thomas Wentworth, the first Earl of Strafford (1672–1739), the additional estates of Boughton and Pitsford in Northamptonshire.

Most of Vyse's life was spent at Stoke Place, a country estate near the village of Stoke Poges in rural Buckinghamshire, England, the extensive grounds of which were designed by the famous English landscape gardener Lancelot "Capability" Brown.

It was very much a life of privilege and patronage in an age when a rigid social structure meant that everyone knew their "station" in life. Vyse was very much from the landed, ruling class—society's elite. A brief glimpse into Vyse's world is provided in *The Court Journal* of 1833, when Vyse's eldest son, Captain George Charles Richard Howard Vyse, upon reaching his twenty-first birthday (his *majority*), held a celebration on the family grounds at Stoke Place.

Saturday August 3rd, 1833
Grand Entertainment at Stoke Park—On Saturday last, Capt. C. H. Vyse, of the 2d Regt. of Royal Horse Guards, attained his majority, when the romantic village of Stoke, near Windsor, was rendered a scene of festivity and rejoicing throughout the day.

The morning was ushered in by the firing of canon in the Park, and the merry peel of the church bells. At one o'clock the children of the charity school in the village, which are entirely clothed and supported by Miss Vyse, were regaled on the lawn. After the dinner, a band of music was stationed on the lawn in front of the house. Numbers of the most respectable tradespeople from Windsor, Eton, and the adjacent villages arrived in the afternoon, and dancing and every other rural sport were kept up with great spirit till late in the evening.

About ten o'clock Capt. Vyse returned to the mansion, and was met on the road by numbers of the peasantry, who took the horses from his carriage, and drew him home amid loud shouts of the multitude.

Immediately on his arrival there was a grand display of fireworks on the lawn, after which the company adjourned to a spacious building in the gardens decorated with laurel and flags and festoons of lamps. On the walls were tastefully displayed the family arms, the initials G.H.V., 21, with the motto "Virtue is more than a thousand shields."

A sumptuous repast was then served up on the lawn; Capt. Vyse took the head of the table, supported by his two brothers of the Royal Blues and Royal Navy. Lord Doneraile gave the health of Capt. Howard Vyse, which was enthusiastically drunk; and the gallant Captain returned thanks in an able and appropriate speech. The convivial scene was kept up till a late hour.[1]

In 1963, after the death a year earlier of Vyse's descendant Major General Sir Richard Granville Hylton Howard-Vyse, the estate of Stoke Place and its grounds were purchased by the South Buckinghamshire District Council, and it is now operated as a hotel and conference center. To this day, however, the house maintains links to its historical owners, with one of the rooms named the Vyse Room.

Being from a wealthy military family with strong links to the British aristocracy, most notably the Duke of Cumberland and the Earl of Strafford, it was expected that Vyse would enter into military service, which he did just before his sixteenth birthday, becoming an ensign in the First Dragoons (the Royal Dragoons), a mounted infantry regiment of the British army. By 1837, Vyse had been promoted to the rank of colonel and finally, in 1846, to the rank of major general.

In 1810, Vyse married his wife, Frances, second daughter of Henry Hesketh, and together they had eight sons and two daughters. Many of Vyse's sons also entered into military service, as was expected of them, most serving with some distinction, although Vyse's youngest son, Captain Francis Howard Vyse, brought some dishonor to the family name when he had to resign from the consular service in Japan after a scandal revealed his activity in illicit artifact dealings.

It seems that Vyse, though having served in the military for much of his life, did not care too much for it, and his passion lay elsewhere, most notably in the field of archaeology. Author Leonard Cottrell, who interviewed a descendant of Vyse, General Sir Richard Howard-Vyse, in the 1950s, writes, "Colonel Richard Howard-Vyse, son of General Richard Vyse (1798–1853), came of a military family, with a country seat at Stoke, in Buckinghamshire. From his writings he appears to have been a man of cultivation, though somewhat deficient in humour and—one suspects— rather a martinet. . . . General Sir Richard Howard-Vyse, descendant of the Colonel, tells me that the great pyramid-explorer was better at archaeology than soldiering, and was 'rather a trial to his family.'"[2]

But Vyse's interest in archaeology would have to be placed on the back burner, for one of the family's other keen interests was in politics, with Vyse and his father having served as Members of Parliament (MPs) in the UK Parliament and Colonel Vyse serving also as the High Sheriff of Buckinghamshire in 1824. It is perhaps this period in Vyse's life that is most revealing, giving us an insight into the character of the man who would later go on to become the first person to present an ancient Egyptian king's name from inside hidden chambers of the Great Pyramid at Giza.

QUESTIONS ABOUT VYSE'S CHARACTER

In 1807, Vyse stood as a parliamentary candidate for the borough of Beverley in the East Riding of Yorkshire. After Vyse won the seat (by a margin not seen before or since), Philip Staple (who finished a very poor third in the contest) presented a petition to Parliament, charging Vyse of electoral fraud.

> A petition of Philip Staple, Esquire, was read, setting forth, That at the late Election for Members to serve in Parliament for the Borough of Beverley, in the County of York, John Wharton, Esquire, Richard William Howard Vyse, Esquire, and the Petitioner, were candidates to represent the said Borough; and that the said John Wharton and Richard William Howard Vyse . . . each of them was guilty of bribery and corruption and corrupt practices in order to their being elected to serve as Members for the said Borough in the present Parliament.[3]

Staple's petition to Parliament was grounded on the Corrupt Practices Act of 1696, which stated that "candidates for election who gave or promised any present or reward to any person having a vote, for the purpose of influencing their vote, shall be declared not elected." This included acts by the candidate themselves, on their behalf, or at their expense through direct or indirect activity. Any candidates found guilty of engaging in or even allowing such behavior on their behalf were to be considered "incapacitated" from serving in Parliament and would not be allowed to take their seat. However, due to inadequacies in the 1696 act, it was strengthened in 1729 and again in 1744.

Staple's petition against Vyse, submitted to Parliament on July 10, 1807 (fig. 3.3, p. 34), was deferred until January 16, 1808, with a decision finally reached by a parliamentary select committee on March 16, 1808. Unfortunately for Staple, the committee did not uphold his petition, declaring Vyse and Wharton duly elected as the two MPs for Beverley. (In 1807, some UK constituencies returned two MPs.)

With the benefit of history, however, it seems that Staple's petition should have succeeded, for it is now known that of the 1,010 votes that Vyse obtained in the 1807 election, a total of 932 of those votes had been secured by Vyse and his agents with monetary bribes. This fact only came to light some sixty years afterward, when, in 1868, a

> 1807   CAPTAIN RICHARD WILLIAM HOWARD VYSE.   1010
>   JOHN WHARTON,   739
>   PHILIP STAPLES. †   279
>
> Plumpers for Vyse, 220 ; Wharton, 136 ; Staples, 17 ; Vyse and Wharton, 559 ; Vyse and Staples, 223 ; Wharton and Staples, 31. Poll, one day. 1203 voted.
>
>   Staples petitioned, July 10th, that Vyse and Wharton, by themselves, friends, and agents, gave to many who pretended to have a right to vote, money, meat, drink, &c., and were also guilty of bribery and corruption. and by gifts, promises. &c., got several to vote for them, and to forbear voting for the petitioner, and by the above, and other illegal and unwarrantable proceedings of Vyse and Wharton and their agents, they got a colourable majority, and were returned to the petitioner's prejudice, who, as he conceived, had a great majority of legal and uncorrupt votes, and was duly elected, and ought to have been returned. The petition was renewed the following session, Jan. 26th, 1808, and the committee declared. March 16th, Wharton and Vyse duly elected, and the petition did not appear frivolous or vexatious, and the opposition of Wharton and Vyse to the petition did not appear frivolous or vexatious.

Fig. 3.3. Staple's petition of electoral fraud against Vyse was rejected by a parliamentary select committee. (Photo: Scott Creighton, from The Parliamentary Representation of the Six Northern Counties of England *by William Wardell Bean)*

parliamentary committee began, once again, to investigate the Beverley parliamentary borough for other alleged claims of electoral corruption. From the investigations of the Beverley Bribery Commission on September 13, 1869, we learn of the sheer scale of Vyse's malpractice during his election campaign of 1807.

> Minutes of Evidence taken before The Beverley Bribery Commission
> Mr. Joseph Hind recalled; examined by Mr. Commissioner Barstow.
>   23,935. What are you, Mr. Hind?—Deputy registrar of deeds for the East Riding of Yorkshire.
>   23,936. How long have you been in Beverley?—All my life.[4]
>   24,055. (Mr. Barstow.) They were all bribed for Keane?—They were all paid 1l [£1]. We do not call it bribery. It is the old customary payment.

24,056. (Mr. Barstow.) Very well, we will distinguish.[5]

24,063. (The witness.) I should like now to explain to the Commissioners the custom which has prevailed with regard to this payment of money. I do not know whether they understand it or not. It has been customary for generations past. I hold in my hand a book of the date of 1807 containing a list of all the persons paid at that election. I should like the Commissioners to know this for the sake of the credit of the borough, as questions have been asked of different witnesses as to how it happens that this system prevails. On the first page of this book there is an entry, "Paying Capt. Vyse's voters, 16th June 1808 [*sic*], R. Dalton." Out of 1,010 who voted for Capt. Vyse it appears from these entries that only 78 did not receive money. For a plumper the amount paid was 3l. 8s [£3 and 8 shillings], and a split vote 1l. 14s [£1 and 14 shillings]. There are several persons who did not vote, for a very good reason, for some of them were in prison. At that time they used to pay wives, grandfathers, grandmothers, uncles, aunts, and everybody connected with them. So that many of these freemen have drunk in the system with their mothers' milk.

24,064. (Mr. Barstow.) What is the authority for these numbers?—It is in the writing of Mr. Frederick Campbell, one of my predecessors and afterward mayor of Beverley; it is partly in his writing and partly in the writing of Mr. Bland; and it is added up in the writing of another of my predecessors, Mr. Atkinson. Mr. Bland was another leading gentleman in the town. You will see that there were several persons paid who did not vote. In fact the system was universal. Everyone took the money. It has been handed down to the present time, the principle of it. I am not mentioning it for the purpose of justifying it, but merely that the Commissioners might have a little consideration.[6]

As is clear from the testimony of the Radical councilor Joseph Hind to the Beverley Bribery Commission in 1869, candidates paying their electorate cash for their vote was not an uncommon practice in rotten boroughs such as Beverley, was a malpractice that extended as far back as Vyse's election of 1807, and was undoubtedly happening even before Vyse's election. Indeed, in 1727, one of the victorious candidates in Beverley was unseated on petition, his agents imprisoned, and, as a result, Parliament was forced to update the Bribery Act. In boroughs such as Beverley, treating and bribery were accepted and even expected parts of parliamentary campaigns, even though, as implied by Hind's testimony, the population and the parliamentary candidates well understood that it was illegal to offer and accept bribes of any kind, being in breach of the Treating Act of 1696 and the Bribery Act of 1729. As historian John Markham explains:

> Men fortunate enough to possess a vote saw it as right and natural that they should be recompensed for their support. Employment, the provision of and payment for nominal duties at elections, patronage and printing orders were all regarded as legitimate demands to make upon a candidate and a necessary and respectable part of his role as a public man. A distinction was clearly drawn by electors between bribery to attract votes and payments and gifts as a *reward* to the loyal supporters of a political party, and those who admitted receiving money often displayed a sophisticated ability to make subtle moral distinctions.[7]

But it also has to be said that not everyone who stood for Parliament was so "morally flexible" or prepared to resort to such unsavory and illegal practices to secure electoral victory. Staple certainly didn't. Hind could not "justify" the electorate of Beverley accepting *rewards* and bribes, for he knew in so doing they were breaking the law of the land. And Vyse would *also* have known and understood that, and, were the truth of his electoral malpractice to have come to light when investigated in 1807 or 1808, he would have struggled to justify his own illegal actions and his electoral success would most likely have been overturned. And even though such corrupt practice was endemic in British elections in this period, simply because others were engaged in such an illegal practice does not make Vyse's actions any less illegal in the eyes of the law—this was a crime punishable by imprisonment.

So in this episode we have our first glimpse into the character of Vyse: that he was a man who would do whatever it took, including perpetrating electoral fraud and spending considerable sums of money to achieve his goal. But what is perhaps even more damning of Vyse in this squalid election of 1807 is that not only did he resort to the illegal act of bribery to secure his victory, but when his methods of securing that victory were later challenged by Staple via a petition to Parliament, Vyse also did not have the good grace, the honor, to confess to Parliament his corrupt practice but instead self-evidently sought to deny any wrongdoing.

It stands to reason that in being successfully appointed as an MP after the parliamentary investigation had concluded, Vyse must surely have denied any wrongdoing to the investigating committee; he must have lied to the British Parliament about any involvement, directly or indirectly, in bribing the electorate in the Beverley election of 1807. Had Vyse openly confessed to his malpractice, then such an admission would have made it quite impossible for the investigating committee to clear his name (as they did), and Vyse most surely would not have been elected to serve as an MP. In short, Vyse won the Beverley contest of 1807 by bribing his electorate and then by denying and lying about it to an investigating committee of the British Parliament.

In 1812, Vyse again stood as a candidate for the UK Parliament, but this time in the seat for Honiton, another rotten borough in East Devon. On this occasion Vyse's election came about as a result of the Honiton seat being uncontested. In Vyse's time two members of Parliament were elected for the Honiton Parliamentary borough. If only two candidates stood then both were automatically elected to Parliament without the need for an electoral contest, elected without a vote even taking place. If, however, there were more than two candidates, this would trigger an election contest in which a vote would have to take place. Voting in this period was not done by secret ballot. In boroughs such as Beverley and Honiton those fortunate enough to possess a vote (universal suffrage was still a long way away in the early nineteenth-century United Kingdom) would often encourage a third person to stand as a candidate, for they knew that only by having a contested election could they hope to gain financially by commanding a price for their vote.

Curiously, the 1812 election in Honiton, one of the most corrupt boroughs in the United Kingdom at that time, went uncontested as the third candidate, Samuel Colleton Graves from the Radical Party, had allowed himself to be waylaid at Taunton, some nineteen miles from Honiton. How this happened isn't exactly clear, but this story does smack of Graves having been induced in some way to withdraw his candidacy. By his not attending the electoral hustings, then there was no third candidate, and, as such, there could be no contest, so both of the other candidates would be automatically elected to Parliament.

Certainly from Vyse's perspective it would have been infinitely easier and much less costly to bribe just *one* individual than almost one thousand, as he had done in the 1807 Beverley election. And if he could successfully "encourage" the third candidate to stand down at Honiton, then there would be much less risk of an awkward electoral petition or investigation to deal with afterward in Parliament.

This is, of course, speculation, and we will likely never know the precise details of this particular election and why Graves "allowed himself to be waylaid." But given Vyse's previous malpractice in the 1807 Beverley election, it surely cannot be ruled out that the colonel's corrupt hand may also have been at work in Honiton and that he perhaps influenced Graves with some form of incentive to stand aside and clear the field for Vyse to be reelected to Parliament uncontested.

Later in his life, during his time at Giza, another charge of fraud was leveled against Vyse, which he presents in his own published book, *Operations Carried On at the Pyramids of Gizeh in 1837*. To wit, "A slanderous paragraph, intended to be inserted in the English newspapers, was this day shown to me, which accused Colonel Campbell of having improperly laid himself under obligations to the Pacha by obtaining the firmaun [a permit to excavate]; and which implied the Colonel and myself intended to make our fortunes under the pretence of scientific researches."[8]

Vyse makes no mention here as to the precise nature of the allegations being made against him. Who exactly was behind these allegations, and what evidence did they have against Vyse? In what way did Colonel

Patrick Campbell improperly obtain the *firmaun* (in this instance, a permit for excavating in the pyramids of Giza that had been issued in the name of the Italian Egyptologist Captain Giovanni Caviglia)? What was the extent of Vyse's involvement? How exactly were the two men planning to make fortunes "under the pretence of scientific researches"? Who was behind these allegations, and what evidence did they have to back them up? While Vyse's published work remains somewhat vague on these key questions and on who precisely it was that made the allegations (though one must suspect the Italian explorer Caviglia after his very public falling out with Vyse), what this episode demonstrates is that someone believed that the activities of Vyse in Egypt were improper, and this individual threatened, via the British press, to expose what Vyse was doing, thus, once again, bringing the moral character of Vyse into question.

Of course, everyone makes mistakes in life, doing things that, upon later reflection, he or she perhaps regrets. So it has to be said that simply because Vyse bribed and lied about his electoral activities of 1807 doesn't mean that everything else he ever did, including his work at Giza, should automatically be considered as somehow corrupt. Vyse's claimed discovery of the painted marks in the hidden chambers may indeed have been entirely genuine. But given the character of the man, a man who was clearly determined to do whatever it took and by whatever means to achieve his ambitions, his claimed discoveries at Giza are surely overcast with a dark shadow. If Vyse had *not* committed electoral fraud and subsequently lied about it to Parliament in 1807, his character would have had little or no bearing on the question of the authenticity of his later claim.

But knowing what we now know of Vyse's character we cannot simply ignore it and pretend that the squalid events of 1807 never happened and have no bearing on the character and credibility of the man and, by extension, the legitimacy of his claimed discoveries in the Great Pyramid.

It is not a case of "once a fraud *always* a fraud" or "once a liar *always* a liar." The point is that had these events of 1807 gone unrecorded and Vyse's character had come down to us unblemished, then his personal character would never have been a factor with regard to his claimed discoveries at Giza. But the simple fact is, that because of his previous malpractice, there *are* question marks over his character, and we simply cannot ignore that. We simply do not know if Vyse is a leopard who managed to change his spots, and given this nagging, lingering doubt, we must surely treat his claimed discoveries at Giza with the appropriate level of caution.

In short, was Vyse's claimed discovery in the Great Pyramid his truest triumph or his darkest deed?

CHAPTER THREE SUMMARY

- Vyse was born into the wealthy, landed gentry, with strong connections to the British aristocracy.
- From the age of fifteen Vyse served in the British military, eventually attaining the rank of major general.
- Vyse was a religious man who had more of a passion for archaeology than he ever did for the military.
- Vyse became the MP for Beverley in 1807, having illegally procured 932 of his votes using monetary bribes. This action was in breach of a number of UK anticorruption and bribery laws.
- Vyse did not disclose his corrupt election practices to the UK Parliament, this coming to light only after a later investigation in 1869, long after Vyse's death.
- The petition against Vyse's election win by Philip Staple, a fellow candidate, was not upheld by the UK Parliament.
- Vyse was elected uncontested to the UK Parliament in 1812 when the third candidate in the Honiton constituency "allowed himself to be waylaid at Taunton."
- An allegation of corruption was made against Vyse during his time at Giza. Vyse does not say who made these allegations.

4

COLONEL VYSE'S CREATION

The questions have to be asked: Why would Vyse have wanted to perpetrate a hoax of this nature within the Great Pyramid, and what, if anything, would he have gained by so doing? Of course, the first thing to say is that we will likely never know with any degree of certainty if the possible motives presented in this chapter were ever actual or active. On this particular question we can but speculate. There are, however, some clues from Vyse's published work that may point to a possible motive for him to perpetrate such a hoax. To understand why Vyse might have been so tempted, it may help us to first understand something of the time and context in which he and his team operated at Giza.

It is difficult for most of us with our twenty-first-century perspective to imagine a time, less than two hundred years ago, when the pyramids of ancient Egypt were barely understood by Western scholars. Only sporadic accounts of them, often colorful and much exaggerated, were relayed back to the parlors and institutions of the great cities of the West by the occasional intrepid European adventurer. Indeed, it was only fifteen years before Vyse arrived at Giza that Jean-François Champollion had published the first-ever translation of Egyptian hieroglyphics along with the grammatical rules to understanding Egyptian writing, a breakthrough that had remained elusive for thousands of years.

This truly was an age of adventure and exploration, the first tentative steps toward a reawakening and rediscovery of humanity's ancient past. But it also has to be said that not all explorers in Egypt in the early to mid-nineteenth century were concerned with the forgotten culture of this most ancient of countries. Some were more interested in whatever treasures they could lay their hands on, treasures that they could sell to wealthy merchants and aristocrats in the West, whose thirst for such precious artifacts seemed insatiable.

As briefly touched on, the story of Vyse's time in Egypt is one loaded with conspiracy and intrigue, of seizing success from the jaws of failure, fierce competition, and not a little corruption and backstabbing.

In 1837, Vyse lived in a world that moved at a much gentler pace, when information could take days or even weeks and months to travel between countries and continents. The first commercial electrical telegraph had only just been invented, while the first trans-Atlantic telegraph cable would not be laid down until 1858. Radio and television were items in Vyse's time that remained in the realms of wild fantasy and extraordinary fiction. The Rocket, an early steam locomotive designed and built by George Stephenson, was at this time only eight years old, and the vast global network of rail tracks that we take for granted today had barely just begun. Photography was in its infancy, which is why many expeditions at this time would take artists along to record significant events and discoveries. It is known, for example, that during his travels across Egypt, Vyse employed the services of the artist Edward James Andrews to make plan drawings of the pyramids and drawings of other features at Giza and beyond.

It was an age when the church still ruled much of everyday life and did so with an iron fist, and its creationist doctrine and religious authority would not be challenged for another twenty-two years, when, in 1859, Charles Darwin would publish his theory of evolution in his seminal work, *On the Origin of Species*.

This was an age of great sailing ships and glorious sea battles, famous battles that Vyse would have held in renown. Indeed, less than forty years previous to Vyse's time in Egypt, in 1798, Lord Horatio Nelson defeated Napoleon Bonaparte's navy at the Battle of the Nile, with the final defeat of Bonaparte by the Duke of Wellington occurring some seventeen years later at Waterloo in 1815. It is little surprise then that Vyse, himself a military man, would dedicate two of the hidden chambers he would discover within the Great Pyramid to these two national heroes of British military history.

In 1837 the final battle of the American Revolutionary War to gain independence from Great Britain had occurred only fifty-four years previously, in 1783, and the first shots of the U.S. Civil War would not occur for another twenty-four years. In the United Kingdom, Queen Victoria would ascend to the throne just one month after Vyse opened Campbell's Chamber, where his claimed discovery of the cartouche of Khufu was found painted on the gabled roof. It is in this distant, bygone age that Vyse lived and worked, and it is within the context of this much-less-connected world where the power and authority of the church held sway that his actions at Giza must be judged.

It is perfectly clear from Vyse's private writings and his published work that he was desperately keen to make an important discovery during his time in Egypt, and in pursuit of this goal he would spend a considerable amount of his personal wealth. Of this desire, he made the following statements in his published book.

- "I wrote to Colonel Campbell from this town, desiring to hear, by a letter directed to Benisouef, whether any discovery of importance had taken place at Gizeh, as, in that case, I intended to return immediately to Cairo, instead of visiting the Faioum."[1]
- "I naturally wished to make some discoveries before I returned to England."[2]
- "I expected to find a sepulchral apartment, to which, I thought it probable, that chamber [Davison's] was an entresol, and the top of the great passage an entrance."[3]
- ". . . extremely desirous, after all the expense incurred, and inconvenience experienced, to endeavor at least to make some discoveries in the Pyramids before I returned to England, which I wished to do without further delay."[4]
- "I still entertained great hopes of finding a sepulchral apartment, and therefore directed that every exertion should be made to get above Wellington's Chamber, for which purpose Daoud [an expert in the use of gunpowder] was employed."[5]
- "All hopes of an important discovery were not given up."[6]

From Vyse's writings it seems clear that he did not consider his discovery of these hidden chambers to be important, for he kept opening them in hopes that in one of these hidden chambers he would find the true sarcophagus of Suphis/Khufu. (The sarcophagus in the main King's Chamber had long been known to have been entirely devoid of any trace of a human burial, leading some to believe that the King's Chamber was perhaps a decoy burial chamber.)

Spurred on by this belief, it seems that Vyse continued on his quest, pinning hope against hope on finding the king's mummy and treasure. No king had ever been found in situ in any pyramid, and if Vyse could have made such a discovery it would have ensured him a place of honor in history, not unlike the international acclaim Howard Carter later gained with his 1922 discovery of the intact underground tomb of Tutankhamen in the Valley of the Kings.

But in the end, Vyse was destined to be somewhat disappointed. After discovering and opening a total of four hidden chambers inside the upper reaches of the Great Pyramid, his great hope was not to be realized; he found no burial chamber, and he certainly did not find the mummified remains of any ancient Egyptian king (or any treasure that would normally have been buried with a king). By the time his operations were completed at Giza, Vyse had spent something in the order of ten thousand British pounds of his personal wealth, which, accounting for inflation, would be equivalent in today's terms to around one million pounds.

Vyse certainly made some notable discoveries during his operations at Giza and sent many artifacts to the British Museum in London. But ultimately he failed in what seems to have been his key personal objective: finding the sepulchre of Suphis/Khufu.

Had Vyse succeeded in his quest he would have proved that the Great Pyramid truly was a tomb and that Khufu, in all likelihood, had it built circa 2550 BCE. And it is on this last point that we must now focus our attention: Could it be that Vyse's quest was not merely to find just any sarcophagus but was, in fact, to find the sarcophagus of Suphis/Khufu in order to *prove* that this ancient king truly was the builder of the Great Pyramid, a find that would give corroboration to the accounts of a number of ancient historians? But why? Why would it have been of any consequence to Vyse to find corroborative proof that this particular ancient king, Suphis/Khufu, was the builder of the Great Pyramid?

As noted earlier, Vyse lived in an age when the Christian Church still had a very strong influence on the daily lives of most people across Europe. And it seems that Vyse, whose great-grandfather was Bishop of Lichfield, was something of a pious man.

Vyse further writes, "Nor can it be recollected without increased interest, that many of those noble monuments, evincing in their construction so much power and skill, and decorated with so many elaborate devices, were raised in very early ages, certainly at no long time after the deluge; and that they therefore not only afford convincing proofs of the refinement, to which mankind had attained before that great event."[7]

He also writes, "On its summit a large school has been established for boys. Similar institutions are to be met with in all the principal towns, and sufficiently prove the Pacha's anxiety to ameliorate by education the condition of his people. Little however can be effected, unless instruction is likewise extended to the females; which, it would appear, can only be accomplished by the introduction of Christianity."[8]

He further states, "It would also appear that castes were established, that brass and iron were manufactured (without which neither wood nor stone could have been worked), and that the arts had arrived at great perfection before the deluge; and it may reasonably be inferred that many of them survived that great event."[9]

Vyse's clear religious outlook was also noted by Leonard Cottrell, who, having interviewed Vyse's descendant in the 1950s, writes, "He was a deeply religious man, with a profound faith in the literal truth of the Old Testament."[10]

Vyse also states, "From the time of Abraham to that of our Saviour the connexion is kept up, chiefly, however, as a prohibited land, in contrast to that of Judea; neither is the extreme state of corruption and of idolatry, into which it afterward fell, at all inconsistent with the supposition that, when most other nations were immersed in darkness, and living in the most savage ignorance, Egypt, and, perhaps, some portions of the East, preserved distinct and accurate traditions of the antediluvian world, originally derived from revelation."[11]

It appears then from the above remarks that Vyse himself was indeed a man of faith and seems to have accepted the Bible as literal fact; the biblical deluge, in Vyse's view, really did take place and appears to have been regarded by him as a matter of historical truth. But not only that, Vyse seems to have *also* held the view that the pyramids themselves were constructed *"certainly at no long time after the deluge."*

Given his apparent certainty of the biblical Flood, it is not unreasonable then to conjecture that Vyse would *also* likely have accepted, unquestioningly, the biblical Creation story and thus that the pyramids must have been built some time *after* the year 4004 BCE, the date that was accepted in Vyse's time (by the calculations of the sixteenth-century Archbishop James Ussher) to have been when the Creation occurred. After all, how could the pyramids or Egyptian writing possibly be older than the Creation?

From Vyse's strong religious convictions we may begin to perceive a possible motive for fraudulent activity at Giza. In 1828 the Catholic Church funded Champollion's first (and only) trip to Egypt on the condition that he would never reveal anything that would contradict the teachings of the church. It is not inconceivable that such anxiety might have been rekindled in the church with Vyse's ongoing discoveries. What if he discovered in those hitherto secret chambers a language never before seen, a language that was not Egyptian and that might be shown to predate the biblical Flood? What if something were discovered in those chambers that could challenge the accepted chronology and truth of the Bible, and possibly even predate the Creation itself? What might such a discovery do to the authority of the church and, of course, to Vyse's personal beliefs? If, on the other hand, Vyse could find a known cartouche of an Egyptian king from the known historical period in one of these newly discovered chambers, an Egyptian king from the *known* Egyptian king lists, written in *known* Egyptian text, then that would effectively prove that the pyramid could never have existed prior to the Flood or the Creation; an outcome that the church would, undoubtedly, have found most satisfactory.

In this regard, Vyse writes, "A cartouche might be found, which would determine the date of the constructions."[12]

As to placing the Khnum-Khuf and Khufu cartouches into these hidden chambers of the Great Pyramid, Vyse would simply have regarded such an act as merely *affirming* what many in his time already held to be true, that Suphis, a known king from the ancient Egyptian king lists, was its builder, thereby firmly locking the structure within the provenance of God's Creation. Vyse may even have regarded his placing of the Suphis/Khufu cartouche into these chambers as undertaking "God's work"; he would be ensuring the authority of the church and, personally, would secure for himself a place of honor in world history books as the man who "found" the Suphis/Khufu name within the Great Pyramid. He would be the man who essentially proved that the Great Pyramid was not older than the Creation, that the last wonder of the ancient world belonged to the second king of the Fourth Dynasty of the ancient Egyptian civilization circa 2550 BCE.

In short, from Vyse's pre-Victorian perspective, the Great Pyramid (and all other pyramids and temples in ancient Egypt) would have made sense to him only in terms of his overarching religious beliefs, beliefs that are now being challenged by twenty-first-century science. And given the powerful influence of such religious beliefs, one might reasonably ponder how the provenance of Göbekli Tepe would have fared had it been discovered in Vyse's time. It is simply inconceivable to imagine that Göbekli Tepe, had it been discovered in 1837, would have been dated to anything remotely like 9500 BCE, the date modern science attributes to this site. In Vyse's time, everything would have had to fit (often forced) into the "religious paradigm" of the Creation date of 4004 BCE.

While this motive remains entirely speculative, we should remember that in the history of humankind many an illegal and immoral act has been perpetrated by people of faith in the name of their religion. The temptation for Vyse to fabricate evidence of the Suphis/Khufu name within the Great Pyramid would have been considerable. As mentioned previously, he had spent a vast amount of his personal wealth in his search for the remains of Suphis but found nothing. There was little of any great importance to show for all his effort and expense, his considerable investment seemingly doomed to become nothing more than a footnote in history—unless, of course, a "miracle" occurred and something important *was* "discovered."

For all the reasons outlined above, if providence was not forthcoming in conferring on Vyse the important discovery he was so clearly desperate to make, then—as his unscrupulous actions to become an MP in the United Kingdom demonstrate—it would be unsurprising if he felt perfectly justified in taking matters into his own hands by giving fate a gentle nudge. And the rest, as they say, is history.

But did Vyse fraudulently place any quarry marks, including the king's various names, within the hidden chambers he discovered and opened? There is a considerable corpus of compelling evidence to suggest that this may well be the case, and we will now consider each of these pieces of evidence in turn, presented in sequential order, commencing at the lowest of the five hidden chambers and working our way up through each chamber toward the topmost and final one, Campbell's Chamber.

CHAPTER FOUR SUMMARY

- Vyse tells us on numerous occasions in his published work that he wanted to make an important discovery during his operations at Giza, possibly even finding the true burial chamber of Suphis/Khufu within the Great Pyramid. Such a discovery would have ensured that his name would have pride of place in world history books.
- Vyse specifically states that finding a cartouche of an Egyptian king within the pyramids might help to date the constructions.
- Given his clear and strong religious beliefs, Vyse may well have wished to ensure that a cartouche was "discovered" within the Great Pyramid that allowed the structure to be dated with a known king from a known historical period; that is, to a time that did not predate Ussher's date of 4004 BCE for the Creation.

5
EXHIBIT 1
OTHER CHAMBERS, OTHER TEXTS

As shown in figure 1.2 (see p. 5) there are a total of five so-called stress-relieving chambers above the King's Chamber of the Great Pyramid. The first of these chambers—the chamber directly above the King's Chamber—was not actually opened by Vyse but was, in fact, discovered some seventy-two years earlier, in 1765, by the British consul to Algiers, Nathaniel Davison. The following account of Davison's discovery is from Robert Walpole's *Memoirs Relating to European and Asiatic Turkey.*

> Nathaniel Davison Esq. was British consul at Algiers: he accompanied Mr. Wortley Montague to Egypt, in the year 1763; resided eighteen months at Alexandria; as many at Cairo; and from that place visited frequently the pyramids of Giza. . . . The merit of the discovery of the room in the Great Pyramid at Giza, over the chamber which contains the sarcophagus, is due solely to Mr. Davison: no traveler before or since his time has examined it; nor has anyone been induced by curiosity to descend so far into another part of the same building.[1]

Curiously, Davison gave no account of any painted marks of any kind having ever been found in the chamber that now bears his name. Caviglia, who made this chamber his living quarters for some considerable time, gave no account of any painted marks therein. Similarly neither of Vyse's assistants, Perring and Hill, or the later archaeologist Alan Rowe—all men who have drawn images of the quarry marks from all the other chambers opened by Vyse—ever made a single drawing of any quarry mark from Davison's Chamber. Zahi Hawass, the former minister of antiquities in Egypt, however, was reported to have observed some painted marks in Davison's Chamber. Hawass undertook an extensive photographic study of all the marks in these chambers in 1996, but he has never made public these photographs.

If there are no obvious quarry marks on the stone walls of Davison's Chamber (as seems to have been testified by no fewer than *six* people— Davison, Caviglia, Vyse, Hill, Perring, and Rowe), why would that be the case? After all, if we consider the profusion of quarry marks in the chambers above Davison's, particularly Lady Arbuthnot's, and the belief by Egyptologists such as Ann Macy Roth that at least two sides of the stone blocks in these chambers would have been painted with the names of the various work gangs at the quarries, then surely, on simple statistical probability alone, at least *some* quarry marks should have been visible on the stone blocks that form the walls, floor, and ceiling of Davison's Chamber.

That no such marks have ever, as yet, been presented remains as peculiar an anomaly today as when Zecharia Sitchin first noted it back in the 1980s. Why should this be? Why is it that the only one of these five relieving chambers that was *not* blasted open with gunpowder by Vyse appears to be the only one that has no painted quarry marks of any kind?

But there is yet another curious aspect to this anomaly. At the end of the southern "star shaft" of the Queen's Chamber (fig. 5.1) a tiny chamber or cavity was discovered beyond a square blocking stone.

In 1993 a small robot named Upuaut II (designed by German engineer Rudolph Gantenbrink) was sent up the southern shaft of the Queen's Chamber, whereupon after an upward journey of some two hundred feet it discovered the blocking stone at the end of the shaft and could go no farther. This blocking stone became known as Gantenbrink's Door. This discovery was followed with another in 2002, when a second robot, Pyramid Rover, was sent up the shaft with

Exhibit 1 • Other Chambers, Other Texts   51

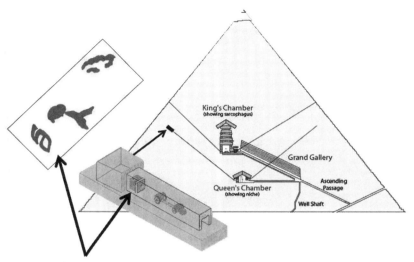

Painted marks found here on floor of small Cavity Chamber at end of Queen's Chamber southern shaft.

Fig. 5.1. The southern shaft-cavity of the Great Pyramid bears red paint marks on the floor of the chamber. (Image: Scott Creighton)

a drill attached to bore through the small blocking stone. The rover was also fitted with a small fish-eye-lens camera that, when pushed through the drilled hole, sent back images of a small cavity with a *second* blocking stone a few inches beyond the first. It wasn't until 2011 that a third robot, Djedi, made the same journey, but this time with an onboard endoscopic camera that when passed through the hole drilled in 2002 was able to twist around to film the walls and the floor of this small recess, revealing some mysterious red-painted symbols located on the floor of this tiny chamber (shown in gray in fig. 5.1).

Independent researcher Luca Miatello, Ph.D., a specialist in ancient Egyptian mathematics, believes the three main symbols on the floor of the shaft-cavity are the numbers 1, 20, and 100, written in old hieratic script (fig. 5.2 on p. 52, *left to right*).

Miatello is tentatively supported in his belief by Zahi Hawass and also by James P. Allen, a professor of Egyptology at Brown University. "The signs are not easy to read, but Miatello's reading is entirely

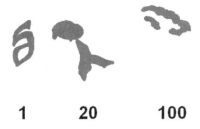

1　　**20**　　**100**

*Fig. 5.2. Reproduction of the painted marks on the floor
of the southern shaft-cavity, which some Egyptologists
believe to be numbers written in old hieratic script.
(Image: Scott Creighton)*

plausible."[2] This is hardly a ringing endorsement from Allen, and his caution is not without reason. A close comparison of the marks with known hieratic signs representing these numerals from the relevant period is far from convincing (fig. 5.3).

As we can see, the signs found in the small shaft-cavity (fig. 5.3, *top*) differ quite substantially from the known hieratic signs (fig. 5.3, *bottom*) that represent the numbers 1, 20, and 100.

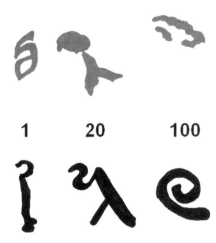

*Fig. 5.3. The shaft-cavity signs (top) believed by Luca
Miatello to be hieratic numerals bear little resemblance
to known Old Kingdom hieratic numeral signs (bottom).
(Image: Scott Creighton)*

Exhibit 1 • Other Chambers, Other Texts   53

But there is a much bigger problem with this discovery. If Miatello is correct and these marks found on the floor of the shaft-cavity (which are obviously authentic ancient marks) are the numerals he claims them to be, written in an early hieratic script, then the orthography of these signs is clearly at odds with the early hieratic quarry marks found by Vyse in the relieving chambers. This is a very peculiar situation indeed, because the highest relieving chamber (Campbell's Chamber) and the small shaft-cavity are at almost the very *same level* within the Great Pyramid and, as such, would have been constructed at the very same time and, presumably, by the same workers, yet two very different styles of old hieratic numerals are presented (figs. 5.4 and 5.5 on p. 54).

If we accept that Miatello is correct, and the signs from the shaft-cavity (fig. 5.5, *top*) represent the numbers 1 and 20, then why is their orthography so radically different from the set of signs from Campbell's Chamber (fig. 5.5, *bottom*), which also represent the hieratic numbers 1 and 20? And why should this be when each set of numbers was, ostensibly, painted into each of these chambers at more or less the same time? Why are the ancient builders simultaneously using two quite different forms of hieratic script to write these numbers? After all, it stands to reason that in a construction project as complex as the Great Pyramid, clear and unambiguous communication of information, most especially numerical measurements, would have been crucial to the success of the project, so we might reasonably expect that a standard form of numerals would have been adopted and deployed throughout every aspect of the construction.

It makes little sense, then, to find numerals written in two quite different hieratic forms, forms that, according to their paleographic evolution, are believed to be separated in time by many centuries (assuming, of course, that the painted marks present in the shaft-cavity are indeed the numeral signs Miatello believes them to be). If, however, Miatello is incorrect in his belief, and it transpires that the painted marks in this tiny chamber are *not* numerals at all, then we may well have an even *bigger* problem on our hands—signs within an inaccessible chamber, written in a script that we simply do not know of, written by

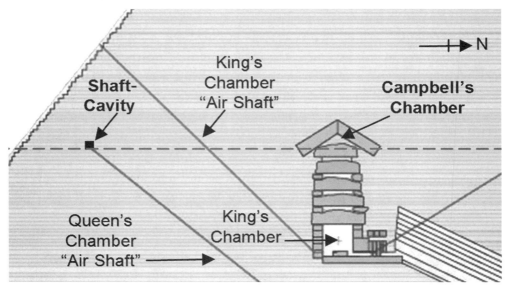

Fig. 5.4. Campbell's Chamber and the shaft-cavity are at the
same level (dotted line) and thus were built at the same time
yet present two radically different styles of old hieratic numerals.
(Image: Scott Creighton)

(Shaft–Cavity numerals)

1　　20

(Campbell's Chamber numerals)

1　　20

Fig. 5.5. The upper hieratic marks (believed to represent the
numbers 1 and 20) were discovered in the shaft-cavity, while the
lower hieratic marks (1 and 20) are claimed to have been
discovered by Vyse on the underside of the gabled roof within
Campbell's Chamber. (Image: Scott Creighton)

Exhibit 1 • Other Chambers, Other Texts   55

people with a language that is much different from that of the ancient Egyptians of the Old Kingdom period that we find painted on the walls and ceilings only of those chambers opened by Vyse.

In short, because no human hand has ever been near any of the painted marks in the small cavity chamber since it was built, we must logically conclude that the written signs within this tiny chamber are indisputably authentic builders' marks. Why then do we not find a similar orthography of the numerals written in Campbell's Chamber, which, being at the same level of the pyramid, would have been constructed at almost the very same time as the small cavity chamber? How can we resolve this contradiction, this conundrum?

One very obvious solution is to simply acknowledge that the different forms of painted numerals we find in these two chambers were created by two very different people, separated by a vast amount of time. Because Campbell's Chamber (and the others below) was accessible to humans after 1837 (and thus to human interference), it would not have been impossible for someone such as Vyse and his team to find and copy what they believed to be appropriate marks into the accessible chambers, which Vyse discovered and opened, believing the marks being copied into those chambers were of a style of ancient Egyptian numerals that was correct for the period; they would have been blissfully unaware that these marks (numerals) would later be found to be inconsistent with a style of numerals that we now know actually *were* undisputedly used by the builders of the Great Pyramid in the small cavity chamber.

It is worth noting here that the very first marks Vyse discovered in Wellington's Chamber (see chapter 6) were (as noted in his private, handwritten journal) unlike the style of the painted hieroglyphic marks he had observed elsewhere at Giza and beyond. All of which is to say that the only chambers to present painted signs that *clearly* belonged to early dynastic Egypt are those discovered and opened by Vyse and his team. All other chambers or cavities thus far discovered in the Great Pyramid that were *not* discovered and opened by Vyse are either completely devoid of any inscriptions or present a style of painted marks that is inconsistent with the style of the painted marks Vyse presented from the four chambers he opened.

This is a highly peculiar situation and one that surely merits further investigation.

CHAPTER FIVE SUMMARY

- The lowest of the so-called stress-relieving chambers of the Great Pyramid was discovered in 1765 by Nathaniel Davison, the British consul to Algiers. Unlike the chambers above, which Vyse would later discover to contain many quarry marks, the chamber that Davison found has not yielded a single quarry mark.

- None of the later explorers of Davison's Chamber has ever produced any markings from it.

- Statistically speaking, we might have expected to find at least some quarry marks in Davison's Chamber.

- In 2011, the robot Djedi, with an onboard endoscopic camera, discovered markings on the floor of the small cavity at the end of the southern shaft from the Queen's Chamber of the Great Pyramid.

- Luca Miatello, a specialist in ancient Egyptian mathematics, believes the markings found by Djedi represent old hieratic signs for the numbers 1, 20, and 100.

- The orthography of the old hieratic signs for the numbers 1 and 20 that were written on the gabled roof blocks of Campbell's Chamber and were claimed to have been discovered by Vyse are entirely different from the old hieratic number signs found by Djedi.

- Given that the small cavity and Campbell's Chamber are at the same level within the Great Pyramid, indicating that they would have been constructed at the same time, it is odd that, in a structure as complex as the Great Pyramid, where numerical standards would have been crucial to the success of the project, the writings in the two spaces present two completely different forms of hieratic numbers (ostensibly) from the very same period.

6

EXHIBIT 2

THE SILENT JOURNAL

It is sometimes the case that a particular truth can present itself by what is *not* stated or what is *not* present in a given situation. We find that such a circumstance arises with an analysis of Vyse's *published* work as compared with the account made by him in his *private* field notes.

If we were to enter Wellington's Chamber, the first and lowest of the four chambers that were discovered, opened, and explored by Vyse (fig. 1.2 on p. 5), we would find two sets of red-painted marks: one set on the east wall (near to the forced entrance to this chamber) and the second set on the west wall. Fortunately, we do not actually have to go all the way to the Great Pyramid and enter Wellington's Chamber to see what the marks actually look like, because Vyse ensured that all the marks on both walls were fully documented by John Shea Perring and J. R. Hill, two of the colonel's closest assistants.

The marks found by Vyse in Wellington's Chamber were the first pieces of writing ever found within *any* of these Old Kingdom pyramids at Giza, and, as such, Vyse would undoubtedly have fully understood the importance and significance of such a discovery. He describes this history-making, pivotal moment of discovery in his published account as follows:

> The hole into Wellington's Chamber being practicable, I examined
> it with Mr. Hill. The floor was unequal, as it was composed of the

reverse of the blocks of granite that formed the ceiling of Davison's Chamber. It was entirely empty, excepting one piece of stone thrown into it by blasting. Not an insect or a bat appeared, nor the traces of any living animal. There had not been, indeed, any doorway or entrance; and although some of the granite blocks in the southern and northern walls had lugs, or projections, yet the stones composing the roof rested upon them—so that it was impossible that they could have been moved up as a portcullis. This chamber, in fact, like Davison's and the others afterward discovered, was merely a vacancy, or chamber of construction, to take off the weight of the building from the King's Chamber. Their dimensions are as follows:—King's Chamber, thirty-four feet three inches, by seventeen feet one inch; Davison's, thirty-eight feet four inches, by seventeen feet one inch; Wellington's, thirty-eight feet six inches, by seventeen feet. In the ceilings alone was any exactness of construction preserved.

These were beautifully polished, and had the finest joints, in order most probably to prevent the slightest accumulation of dust

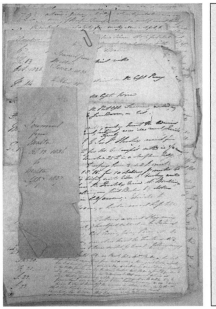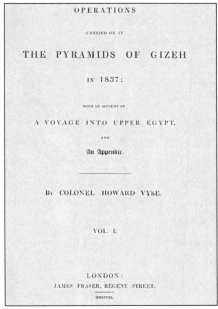

Fig. 6.1. Vyse's private journal (left) and published book (right)
(Image: Scott Creighton)

Exhibit 2 • The Silent Journal 🦉 59

or of rubbish. In all other respects, the masonry in these apartments became less perfect as they ascended. The northern and southern walls of Wellington's and of Davison's Chambers were of granite, the eastern and western of calcareous stone; the ceiling consisted of nine blocks of granite laid from north to south, and were, like those in Davison's apartment, of a sufficient length to extend their bearings beyond the walls of the King's Chamber. The average height of the chamber (which varies, owing to the irregular surface of the floor) was about three feet eight inches. Mr. Perring, in the course of his survey, found that these apartments had been finished from the eastward, and that consequently the western sides were last built.

For a day or two after the chamber had been opened, those who remained in it became blackened as if by a London fog: as this effect gradually disappeared, I conceive it to have been occasioned by blasting, and by the sudden admission of the air. Upon first entering the apartment, a black sediment was found, of the consistence of a hoar-frost, equally distributed over the floor, so that footsteps could be distinctly seen impressed on it, and it had accumulated to some depth in the interstices of the blocks. Some of this sediment, which was sent to the French establishment near Cairo, was said to contain igneous particles. When analyzed in England, it was supposed to consist of the exuviae of insects; but as the deposition was equally diffused over the floor, and extremely like the substance found on the 25th instant at the Second Pyramid, it was most probably composed of particles of decayed stone. If it had been the remains of rotten wood, or of a quantity of insects that had penetrated through the masonry, it would scarcely have been so equally distributed; and, if caused by the latter, it is difficult to imagine why some of them should not have been found alive when the place was opened evidently for the first time since the pyramid was built.

Having ordered the entrance to be enlarged, I went round the other works. I afterward wrote to Colonel Campbell, and sent with my letter the idols found in his tomb. Mr. Perring and Mr. Mash having arrived, we went in the evening into Wellington's Chamber, and took various admeasurements, and in doing so we found the quarry marks.[1]

As we can see from Vyse's account, he and his team examined this chamber fairly thoroughly upon their first visit, yet it seems that it was only upon their *second* visit to Wellington's Chamber (on the evening of the same day it was first opened, March 30, 1837) that the "quarry marks" were found. Oddly, Vyse does not present in his published volumes any details of the actual quarry marks that were found in this chamber. However, on May 9 of that year, Vyse instructed Hill to make 1:1 facsimile drawings of the marks in the chambers they had thus far opened (which are now deposited in the British Museum). While Hill recorded only the quarry marks on the west wall of Wellington's Chamber (a gang name with its cartouche), Perring, as part of his plan survey, made drawings of the quarry marks found on the east *and* west walls of Wellington's Chamber (fig. 6.2).

In Perring's drawing of the painted marks from the east wall of

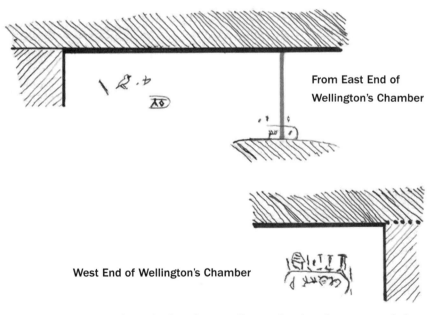

Fig. 6.2. Painted marks found in Wellington's Chamber as recorded by J. S. Perring. Note the small bird beside some geometric marks and partial cartouche with vertical line (top left, east wall) and the upside-down gang name with its cartouche (bottom, west wall). (Image: Scott Creighton based on original drawing by J. S. Perring)

Exhibit 2 • The Silent Journal 🏛 61

Wellington's Chamber (fig. 6.3), we observe a small bird alongside some other marks (geometric shapes in a partial oblong). These marks do not appear like typical ancient Egyptian hieratic script, while the quarry marks drawn by Perring and Hill from the chamber's west wall (fig. 6.4), although somewhat sketchy, present a gang name that bears the royal cartouche of Khnum-Khuf (believed to be Khufu's full birth name) written in old hieratic script.

Fig. 6.3. Enlarged section of Perring's drawing (east wall) of a bird with some geometric marks close by (Image J. S. Perring)

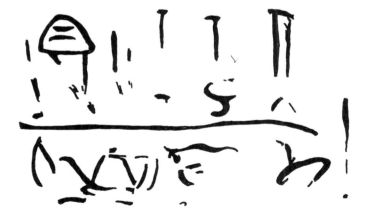

Fig. 6.4. Artist's impression of quarry gang name with associated Khnum-Khuf cartouche in Wellington's Chamber (west wall). (Image: Scott Creighton, based on original drawing by J. R. Hill)

It is worth noting here that Vyse would frequently interchange the term "quarry marks" with the word "hieroglyphics." In 1837 few would have made the distinction we make today between painted quarry marks of hieratic script and sculpted hieroglyphics. To Vyse these red-painted signs (i.e., hieratic quarry marks) were simply painted hieroglyphics. The painted geometric marks on the east wall of this chamber, however, are unusual, being unlike typical hieratic or hieroglyphic signs.

Because Vyse makes no mention in his published account of any additional painted marks having been found in Wellington's chamber at any later date, we are thus obliged to accept (according to his published account) that *all* of the marks on the east *and* west walls of this chamber, including the partial cartouche (on the east wall) and the full gang name with its associated cartouche (on the west wall), constitute the totality of the "quarry marks" Vyse states were found in Wellington's Chamber on the evening of March 30, 1837.

But just how accurate is this official account?

Oddly, while Vyse's published book states simply, "we found the quarry marks," thereby implying that *all* of the marks from Wellington's Chamber (including the partial cartouche on the east wall and the full gang name and its associated Khnum-Khuf cartouche on the west wall) were found on the evening of March 30 (his second visit to this chamber), his *private* diary of the very same evening paints a quite different picture. Thanks to a brief, online collaboration[2] with independent researcher Martin Stower, the events of this momentous evening were transcribed from Vyse's cryptic handwriting: "In Wellington's Chamber, there are marks in area of the stones like quarry marks of red paint, also the figure of a bird near them, but nothing like hieroglyphics."

And that is it. Vyse's private account (fig. 6.5) of his second visit to this chamber (with Perring and Mash) makes no mention of any identifiable quarry marks in this chamber and, remarkably, makes no mention whatsoever of *any* royal cartouche (partial or otherwise) having been found—just red marks that are *like* quarry marks (i.e., the red-painted geometric marks with the figure of a bird near them, fig. 6.3). Note also Vyse's use of the word "area" (singular). Had Vyse also found the quarry

Exhibit 2 • The Silent Journal 63

Fig. 6.5. Extract from Vyse's private journal, March 30, 1837
(Photo: Scott Creighton)

marks on the west wall of this chamber at this time (as he implies in his published account) then wouldn't he surely have written "areas" (plural) in his private account?

So, while Vyse's published book simply tells us that on the evening of March 30, 1837, "quarry marks" were found (without ever specifying *which* quarry marks), his private journal speaks *only* of the marks on the east wall near the entrance (and says that the marks he found looked "nothing like hieroglyphics," i.e., nothing like the usual red-painted quarry marks he would have been familiar with). And it is worth repeating—in this account there is absolutely no mention of *any* cartouche having been found in this chamber. Clearly then, Vyse's private and published accounts are somewhat at odds with each other, and we have to ask why that would be; why does Vyse's *published* account state "we found the quarry marks" and yet his *private* account states he found "nothing like hieroglyphics" (i.e., nothing like typical red-painted hieratic quarry marks)?

This is all the more puzzling because, among the painted marks on the east wall of Wellington's Chamber, we find a partial cartouche, and those on the west wall of Wellington's Chamber present the *very first* full royal cartouche of a king ever found in any of these pyramids—painted quarry marks that Vyse most certainly *would* have regarded as "hieroglyphics"—an important discovery that would have given Vyse what he craved: a discovery that would ensure his place of honor in the world's history books. Yet Vyse makes no specific mention of these marks, of this king's cartouche, whatsoever in either his private or published accounts. There is no "cartouche found!" moment in Vyse's private journal. Instead, Vyse, through his vague statement in his published account, merely *implies* that the partial cartouche on the east wall and the gang name (with its all-important cartouche) on the west wall was among the quarry marks that were found.

Again, we have to ask *why?* Why is the elephant missing from the room, so to speak? In consideration of this question it seems that there are two possible scenarios to explain why Vyse neglected to make any mention in his private journal or in his published book of these highly prized quarry marks, in particular the king's cartouche on the west wall of Wellington's Chamber.

1. The gang name with its all-important cartouche was present on the west wall of the chamber when Vyse and his team first entered but was overlooked by everyone during their extensive examination of this chamber and perhaps was only discovered sometime afterward, although no such later discovery is ever explicitly stated in any of Vyse's accounts.
2. The gang name with its prized cartouche was not present on the west wall of this chamber on the evening of March 30, 1837 (contrary to its implied presence in Vyse's published account). So the glyphs on the west wall (and the partial cartouche on the east wall) must, therefore, have been placed there sometime *afterward* by Vyse and/or his assistants.

What Vyse states in his published account about this date is, of course, quite true; he *did* find marks in Wellington's Chamber (those on the east wall), but when we consider the details of the discovery he relates in his private account, it appears that he *did not* discover the west wall marks (gang name with its cartouche), possibly because these particular marks simply were not yet in the chamber at this time. Why then does Vyse, in his published account, imply that *all* the quarry marks in this chamber (east and west walls) were discovered *at the same time,* when, according to his private account, they evidently were not? Why does he say in his published account that "the quarry marks were found" and yet his private account tells us he found nothing like hieroglyphics (i.e., red-painted quarry marks of

Exhibit 2 • The Silent Journal   65

hieratic script)? Is this a case of Vyse "lying by obfuscation," fudging the extent and truth of his discovery in his published account through the use of vague language, language that allows him to be economical with the truth and that, it has to be said, presents him with a measure of plausible deniability?

So here we have our first hint that all may not be what it seems in Vyse's published account of his claimed finding of the quarry marks in the four hidden chambers he opened. While this contradiction between private and published accounts may not, of itself, prove any wrongdoing, it most certainly does raise a number of legitimate questions: Why does Vyse fail to mention the major discovery of a royal cartouche in his private account of March 30, 1837, then imply its discovery on this date in his published account? Why the lack of clarity, the obfuscation? And why did he omit all the quarry marks found in this chamber from his published work when these hieroglyphs—particularly the cartouche of the king's name—reveal the very first royal name *ever* to have been found inside *any* of these pyramids?

As previously stated, the discovery of this cartouche alone would have given Vyse what he so clearly sought—a cartouche that would allow the dating of the constructions—but on this matter Vyse's private journal remains strangely silent. If nothing else, this is very peculiar behavior indeed.

After Wellington's Chamber, Vyse went on to blast his way into three more hidden chambers within the Great Pyramid and to discover what he describes in his published account simply as "quarry marks" or "a great many quarry marks." Among these other quarry marks Vyse would find a number of other royal cartouches of Khnum-Khuf and one complete cartouche of Khufu. This is surely an odd way to describe the discovered cartouches, because Vyse:

A. explicitly states that he was in search of a cartouche that might help to date the structure, and

B. draws and makes reference to the cartouche of Suphis/Khufu several times in his *private* field notes. He absolutely knew during his time in Egypt what a cartouche was, its importance to his own particular quest, and certainly how the Suphis/Khufu cartouche should look.

And yet, for all of this, in his published book Vyse describes the royal cartouches he allegedly found simply as "quarry marks," conferring upon them no more import than any of the other quarry marks discovered, creating the impression in the reader's mind that he is wholly ignorant and blissfully unaware of the historical significance of the royal cartouches.

It is almost as if Vyse, in his published account, has somehow lost all his prior knowledge of what a cartouche is and their importance to his quest; it seems that the painted cartouches he found are all now just meaningless quarry marks to him. However, from his private journal it is perfectly clear (as we shall see in chapter 13) that Vyse well understood that a number of cartouches were among the quarry marks he had Hill make facsimile copies of and had afterward sent to the experts at the British Museum, yet in his published account he makes no specific mention of having identified *any* cartouche from these chambers. There is no "eureka!" moment, no entry in his published account (or private account) saying something like, "Today among the quarry marks the cartouche of Suphis was discovered."

And we have to ask *why not?* Why does Vyse, in his published account, defer to Samuel Birch of the British Museum to make the identification of the Khnum-Khuf and Khufu cartouches among all the facsimiles of quarry marks sent from Giza? Why, in his published account, is Vyse being so coy, so shy about coming forth with his own knowledge, particularly of the Suphis/Khufu cartouche? Why the pretense in his book that he knows little if anything of the marks he had found in these chambers when his *private* journal clearly shows that he most certainly *did* recognize the Suphis/Khufu cartouche and, of course, would have well understood its significance to his quest? In short, why, in his published account, is Vyse going out of his way to understate his own knowledge of the quarry marks he claims to have found, knowledge that is so clearly evident in his *private* account?

It is certainly odd behavior on the part of Vyse. Of course, were Vyse to have presented himself in his published book as having little

Exhibit 2 • The Silent Journal 67

knowledge of what the quarry marks he claims to have found actually represented, then no one could ever accuse him of fabricating the marks himself. After all, how could he possibly have fabricated the Suphis/Khufu cartouche in the Great Pyramid if he is seen as having little knowledge of what the quarry marks were, let alone knowing that among the quarry marks there were to be found the various names of an ancient Egyptian king?

Of course, if this were the only question that Vyse's private and published accounts raised, then the case of forgery in the Great Pyramid would be a very thin case indeed. There are, however, many more facts to be unfolded in the forthcoming pages of this book, and these further facts raise many other legitimate questions regarding the provenance of these marks Vyse claimed to have discovered.

CHAPTER SIX SUMMARY

- Vyse entered Wellington's Chamber (the first chamber to be discovered and opened by him) on March 30, 1837. He entered the chamber a second time on the evening of the same day with two of his assistants. It was during this evening visit, Vyse tells us in his published account, that the quarry marks were found. Vyse does not specify in his published account precisely which marks were found, thereby implying that *all* quarry marks subsequently presented from this chamber were found at the same time.

- Vyse's private journal speaks only of marks found on the east wall of the chamber, some odd geometric signs near the figure of a bird, and states that the marks in this area looked "nothing like hieroglyphics."

- In his private account Vyse makes no mention of finding the Khnum-Khuf cartouche on the west wall of this chamber, a discovery that is implied in his published account. This is an odd omission given that this is precisely what Vyse tells us in his published book he was hoping to find: "A cartouche might be found, which would determine the date of the constructions." The elephant is missing from the room.

- Given also his desire to make an important discovery, it is very odd indeed that Vyse makes no mention in his private journal of finding this royal cartouche in Wellington's Chamber—the *first* ever royal cartouche within the Great Pyramid and thus a highly important event indeed that would have ensured Vyse a place in the history books.

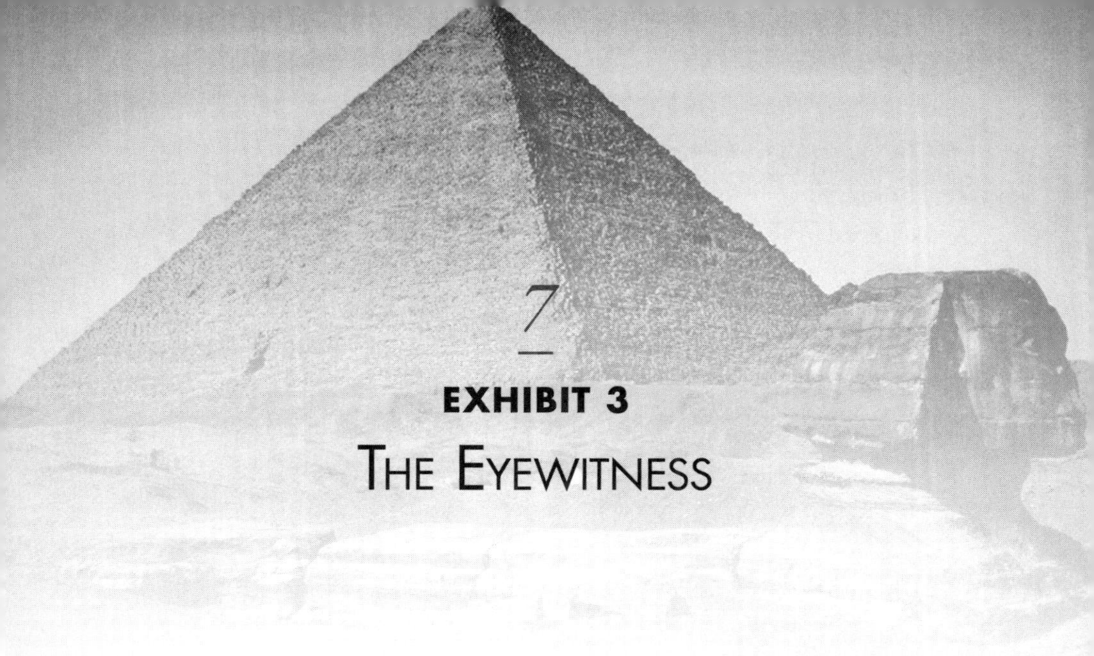

7

EXHIBIT 3

THE EYEWITNESS

In any investigation, civil or criminal, one thing that investigators always seek is a reliable eyewitness. The eyewitness account of the events can help to corroborate a particular set of circumstances and can often be the decisive factor when there is more than one competing version of a particular event.

As outlined in chapter 1, in his 1980 book *Stairway to Heaven,* Zecharia Sitchin first put forward the controversial claim that the painted marks found by Vyse in the four stress-relieving chambers of the Great Pyramid had been forged by Vyse with the assistance of two of his closest assistants, Hill and Perring.

While much of the evidence Sitchin presented in support of his controversial claim has been, as a result of inadequate research, comprehensively debunked, there are certain aspects of his original investigation that remain valid even to this day, pieces of evidence presented by Sitchin that have never, as yet, been satisfactorily answered.

One such piece of evidence (eventually published in Sitchin's 2007 book, *Journeys to the Mythical Past*) was a copy of a page from the radio logbook belonging to Walter Martin Allen, a ham radio enthusiast and amateur genealogist, which Allen had sent to Sitchin some years earlier.

In *Journeys to the Mythical Past,* Sitchin writes of this contact by Allen.

In May 1983, three years after *The Stairway to Heaven* was published, I received an astonishing letter. It was from a Mr. Walter M. Allen of Pittsburgh, Pa. "I have read your book," he [Walter Allen] wrote. "What you say about the forgery in the Cheops pyramid was not new to me." His great-grandfather, he wrote, was an eyewitness to the forgery!

"I have your letter of May 7th and am literally flabbergasted," I [Sitchin] wrote him back. "That my conclusion could be supported by a virtual eye-witness was beyond my wildest expectations!" . . . He signed it "Walter M. Allen. AFTER 150 YEARS"[1]

Allen had learned of Sitchin's pyramid forgery theory in late March 1983 through his interest in *The Unexplained,* a weekly mysteries column written by George Cunningham-Tee for the *Pittsburgh Press*. In his column Cunningham-Tee had outlined Sitchin's pyramid forgery theory (from *The Stairway to Heaven*), and this revelation so resonated with Allen that it prompted him to contact Sitchin directly, explaining to the author that while he had been researching his family's history in 1954, he had come across information (from discussions with his mother and some family elders) that his great-grandfather Humphries Brewer had actually worked with Vyse and his team at Giza in 1837.

As he discussed his great-grandfather's life with his elderly relatives, Allen took notes, writing the key details of their discussions (which included some family letters from his great-grandfather's time) into some blank pages of his radio logbook (fig. 7.1).

The following is a transcription of figure 7.1's handwritten text from Allen's logbook (all spelling and punctuation as entered in the logbook).

Sat Oct 9 1954 Johnstown with mother. Her visit Corning with Nell Pattengill August. Also to settle grandpa's estate in Bath N.Y.

Visited uncle Mac in hospital. Went to Watkingsglen [Watkin's Glen] And Addison. Catherine saw house at Addison. Mother was born there. She will be 78 next month. Nell had some of Humfreys letters & Wm Brewers letters from England. Got them from her father Wm Marchant Brewer.

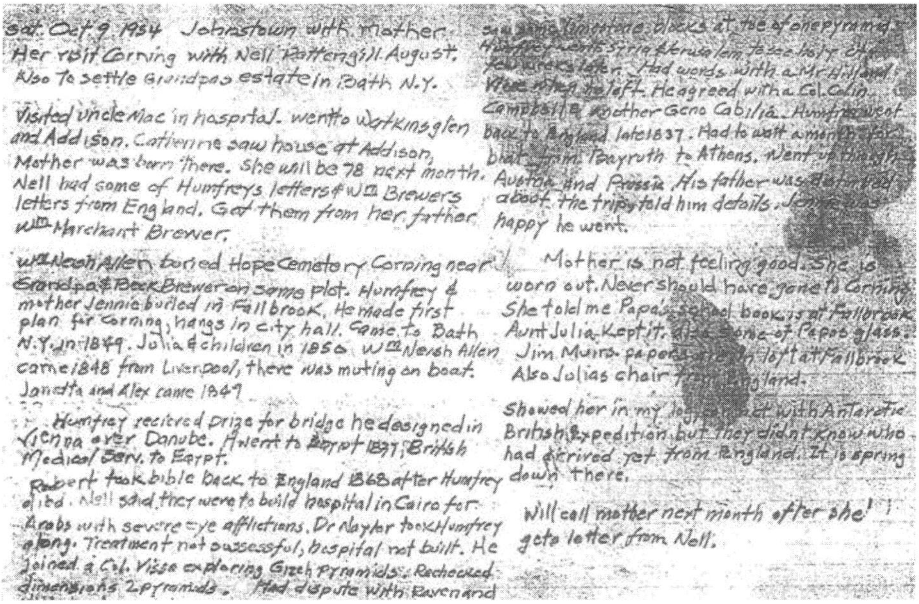

Exhibit 3 • The Eyewitness   71

Fig. 7.1. Logbook entry of Walter Allen dated Saturday, October 9, 1954, citing his great-grandfather Humphries Brewer and his apparent eyewitness account of forgery at the Great Pyramid in 1837. (Image from Journeys to the Mythical Past by Zecharia Sitchin)

Wm Neish Allen buried Hope Cemetery Corning near Grandpa & Beck Brewer on same plot. Humfrey & mother Jennie buried in Fallbrook. He made first plan for Corning, hangs in city hall. Came to Bath N.Y. in 1849. Julia & children in 1850. Wm Neish Allen came 1848 from Liverpool, there was mutiny on boat. Janetta and Alex came 1849.

Humfrey received prize for bridge he designed in Vienna over Danube. H went to Egypt 1837, British Medical Serv. to Egypt.

Robert took bible back to England 1868 after Humfrey died. Nell said they were to build hospital in Cairo for Arabs with severe eye afflictions. Dr. Naylor took Humfrey along. Treatment not sussessful, hospital not built. He joined a Col. Visse exploring Gizeh pyramids. Rechecked dimensions 2 pyramids. Had dispute with Raven and Hill about painted marks in pyramid. Faint marks were repainted, some were new. Did not find Tomb.

Saw some limestone blocks at top of one pyramid. Humfrey went to Syria & Jerusalem to see holy city few weeks later. Had words with a Mr. Hill and Visse when he left. He agreed with a Col. Colin Campbell & another Geno Cabilia. Humfrey went back to England late 1837. Had to wait a month for boat from Bayruth [Beirut] to Athens. Went up through Austria and Prussia. His father was disturbed about the trip, told him details. Jennie was happy he went.

Mother is not feeling good. She is worn out. Never should have gone to Corning. She told me Papa's school book is at Fallbrook. Aunt Julia kept it. also some of Papas glass. Jim Muirs papers are in loft at Fallbrook. Also Julias chair from England.

Showed her in my log contact with Antarctic British Expedition but they didnt know who had arrived yet from England. It is spring down there.

Will call mother next month after she gets letter from Nell.

The controversial aspect of Allen's 1954 logbook entry lies at the foot of the first column, where he writes:

He joined a Col. Visse exploring Gizeh pyramids. . . . Had dispute with Raven and Hill about painted marks in pyramid. Faint marks were repainted, some were new. Did not find Tomb.[2]

Evidently, from this eyewitness account passed down in family letters, two of Vyse's closest assistants, Raven and Hill, were painting new marks in the Great Pyramid and painting over some faint marks that were already there. And it seems that Brewer, Allen's great-grandfather, took exception to the actions of Raven and Hill and had a dispute with them about what they were doing. Allen's account further states:

Had words with a Mr. Hill and Visse when he left. He agreed with a Col. Colin Campbell & another Geno Cabilia.[3]

So here we have in Allen's logbook page the names of many of the key players at Giza in 1837, albeit with some misspellings of the less common

Exhibit 3 • The Eyewitness   73

or obvious names (to be expected in a semi-oral tradition). Ideally, of course, it would have been preferable to have had access to the original family letters that Allen's logbook entry was based on, but although he tried to locate these documents some thirty years after first penning his logbook entry, it is unsurprising that they were not to be found. As matters stand, all that we are left with is the brief account, written by Allen himself based on his discussions with family elders in 1954.

Bizarrely, in an attempt to debunk the account of Allen, skeptics have made various allegations to the effect that Brewer (because of his complete absence in Vyse's published work) wasn't a real person and even that the personage of Allen was but a fabrication (presumably by Sitchin) and that this eyewitness account was entirely fabricated in order to corroborate Sitchin's forgery claim. But that is absolutely not the case, as it can be shown that both Humphries Brewer and Walter Allen are verifiable people and that they were indeed of the same family.

Humphries Brewer was born in the Parish of Box, Wiltshire, England, on February 28, 1817, and studied in London to become a civil engineer. He married Julia Orton in 1846, and the couple moved from England to America in 1849, settling in the small community of Fallbrook in Pennsylvania, where Brewer became the manager of the Fallbrook Mining Company. After a very successful career, Brewer's life was tragically cut short when he died in 1867, aged just fifty years.

Here we have Brewer's obituary from the *Watkins Express,* January 16, 1868.

𝔚𝔞𝔱𝔨𝔦𝔫𝔰 𝔈𝔵𝔭𝔯𝔢𝔰𝔰

JANUARY 16, 1868

DEATH OF HUMPHRIES BREWER— We copy, by request, the following obituary notice from the *Wellsboro Herald:*

It is with a melancholy feeling that we announce the death of Humphries Brewer. We cannot suffer the occasion to pass without passing some feeble tribute to the memory of one who was endeared to almost every person with whom he has ever been associated. His sudden and untimely death has fallen with crushing weight on the hearts of his family and friends; as well as upon the business public in this county. The place he occupied is now a blank. The commanding position to which he had carved his way, will long wait for a claimant. Though not an old man he had earned a name for business ability, and enjoyed a reputation amongst the many persons with whom he had been associated that few persons have been fortunate enough to win.

Humphries Brewer was born in the Parish of Box, Wiltshire, England and died on the 25th day of December last, aged 50 years, 9 months and 27 days.

The writer of this article is not sufficiently acquainted with the earlier parts of his life to give a correct history of it. Enough, however, is known of it to state that he had the advantages of early training; that he was thoroughly educated in all the higher branches of mathematics; and that he was an accomplished geologist before he came to this country.

He had also traveled through Egypt and the Holy Land, and his mind was well stored with an accurate knowledge of the history of that portion of the Old World.

He emigrated to this country some twenty years ago; since which time he has resided at Blossburg and Fall Brook. His knowledge of geology led him into this locality, and he began to make early examinations into the coal deposits in and about Blossburg. The summers of 1857 and 1853 were mostly spent by him and Mr. D. S. Magee in making explorations upon the land where Fall Brook now stands. The location of the first drift; the plan of the Rail road from Blossburg to Fall Brook; the construction of the Schutes, platforms and other coal fixtures were all the fruits of his energy and will. In fact Fall Brook with its immense interest has all grown up under his nurture and care; not a blow has been struck, not an improvement made except under his direction. In less than ten years he has changed it from a barren and rugged wilderness to a place of immense business and great productive wealth.

Hundreds of men are constantly there. It has opened one of the best markets in the county, and disbursed thousands of dollars monthly, among the people.

Mr. Brewer united with his other qualities that of an accomplished engineer. In the intricate and difficult business of the mining and railroad interests this was a most valuable qualification. He was also an ingenious mechanic, and has left behind as an evidence of it many valuable

Exhibit 3 • The Eyewitness 75

inventions at Fall Brook. In his business character we find that assemblage of virtues which made him so invaluable. He possessed what is rarely found in business men, in combination, clear perception, great energy, and great caution. Blessed with an almost instinctive perception of character, he read men at a glance. The business he controlled at different times would have employed several common men; yet he was enabled by the energy and power of his mind to so guide and control it, that it appeared to be easy and smooth. Mr. Brewer was an honest man and constantly trusted with thousands; placed where his name was law, and where his judgment dictated what was right between his fellow men. Yet he has gone to his grave without a stain of dishonesty upon him. No man has said, no person will ever say that he wronged them. His heart was always warm and generous. There are hundreds that gratefully blessed him while he lived, and we know (for we have heard) many of the poor and dependent bemoan his loss with tears in their eyes. He was just, manly, and natural in all he did. Free from flattery and mockish sensibility, it may be truly said that no man was ever deceived by him. He was taciturn in business, but always truthful.

We shall miss him in Fall Brook, when we go there. The people of Wellsboro and Cowanesque will miss his counsels and his energy in the improvements which were soon to be made under his guidance. But above all will his family and his intimate friends, who were in daily intercourse with him, miss him in the social relations. To them he was beloved as few men are; but he rests in the bosom of his mother earth, upon the rugged mountain where he spent the last years of his life, in the midst of a population that depended upon and loved him; where the strongest efforts of his life had been made, and with all the associations and landmarks of his own late efforts about him. He is a part of Fall Brook. She is the production of his genius and it is well that he should sleep here.

So clearly Humphries Brewer was a very real and highly regarded individual, and as we can see from his obituary, he did indeed travel to Egypt in his early life. But what of Allen and his relationship to Brewer? What do we know about that?

As indicated briefly in this chapter, Allen was something of an amateur genealogist, spending much of his time researching his family

Fig. 7.2. This photo of Walter Allen and family members, from the Pittsburgh Press, *was captioned "Mrs. Mary Ann Lipsman, her daughter, Heather, 8, and father, Walter Allen, are excited about the way their family tree is branching out."*

history (fig. 7.2). This 1977 article from the *Pittsburgh Press* (later the *Pittsburgh Post-Gazette*) gives us a little insight into Allen's interest in tracing his family roots and shows that this was a passion he had for much of his life, passing that interest on to his daughter and granddaughter.

> Mary Ann Allen-Lipsman is "putting flesh on the bones" of her ancestors.
>
> Mrs. Lipsman of Mt. Lebanon is one of hundreds of Western Pennsylvanians checking family stories in libraries, archives, churches, and courthouses to find the roots and fill out the branches of a family tree.
>
> Seven years of research have taken her and her father, Walter Allen of Bethel Park, as far back as 1300 in one branch.

Exhibit 3 • The Eyewitness 77

It also took them as far away as the British Isles in a three-week "genealogical safari" two years ago.

"We wanted to find out who our ancestors were, how they suffered, why they came to the United States and under what conditions they arrived," Allen said.

"We found rebels in the (*second*) Jacoby Rebellion in Scotland (*in 1745*) who deserted and were wanderers in fear of savage execution," Allen said. "We found rebels in the 1798 Irish Rebellion. We found a few were executed. We found fishermen and cattle drovers."

One of their ancestors, Humphries Brewer, came to Pennsylvania in 1849 and made the first major discovery of semibituminous coal in Fall Brook, now a ghost town in Tioga County.[4]

(Excerpted from the *Pittsburgh Press.* Copyright *Pittsburgh Post-Gazette,* 2015, all rights reserved. Reprinted with permission.)

As we can see from this *Pittsburgh Press* article, Humphries Brewer is identified as one of Walter Allen's ancestors and arrived in America in 1849. There is no doubt, then, that both Brewer and Allen were real people and that they were related. As such, it is not unreasonable to expect that a story from Brewer of forgery occurring during his time working with Vyse at the Great Pyramid could very well have survived and been passed down the generations in written and oral forms to eventually reach Allen, who would finally commit the account to his logbook.

The difficulty with all of this, as briefly stated above, is that in Vyse's book *Operations Carried on at the Pyramids of Gizeh in 1837* there is a complete absence of Brewer's name; there is not a single mention of this individual anywhere in Vyse's published work. This glaring absence has prompted a number of skeptics to question the credibility of Allen's logbook account, inferring that the whole Brewer story is itself some elaborate hoax perpetrated to corroborate Sitchin's forgery claim. And given that Allen's logbook account was not published until 2007 in Sitchin's *Journeys to the Mythical Past,* some seven years after Allen's death, the chief suspect of this alleged hoax is Sitchin himself.

This suspicion exists despite both Allen and Sitchin appearing on the same Pittsburgh radio show in 1983 discussing the pyramid forgery claim and Allen's logbook confirmation of it from his great-grandfather. We are also expected to believe that Sitchin would falsify something about Allen's great-grandfather Humphries Brewer in one of his books, something that Allen's surviving family could have very easily discovered and called foul. Sitchin would have been very silly indeed to have even contemplated such a thing, let alone to carry it out.

But still the skeptics refuse to accept the Allen logbook account as a credible piece of evidence. This skepticism is typified by the authors Ian Lawton and Chris Ogilvie-Herald, who write in their book, *Giza: The Truth:*

> So the only "family records" that apparently still exist are those in Allen's logbook. The real contemporary evidence, the letters supposedly written by Brewer to his father, have never been produced, either to Sitchin or by him. Sitchin asserts that dates, names and other data corroborate these claims. Yet we know that Vyse was scrupulous in recording the names and activities of his senior staff, and also meticulous about giving credit for important discoveries to those involved, even if, as in the case of Caviglia, he had already fallen out with them. Since Brewer was apparently "the very stonemason from England whom Col. Vyse engaged to use gunpowder inside the pyramid" (Sitchin's words), it is surely appropriate to ask why his name is entirely absent from the three volumes of Vyse's *Operations Carried on at Gizeh.* And unless Sitchin can come up with better evidence than this—at the very least the contents of the logbook, verified by an independent witness and preferably scientifically tested to authenticate its date—it is inadmissible.[5]

In fairness (as stated previously), it would indeed have been preferable to have had access to the original testimonies and/or documents on which Allen based his logbook notes. As matters stand, the explosive content of Allen's logbook, without some kind of corroboration, amounts to little more than hearsay. The story may well be true, but without something to authenticate it, it is destined to simply be ignored

Exhibit 3 • The Eyewitness 79

by mainstream Egyptology. In the words of Lawton and Ogilvie-Herald, this particular piece of evidence will be regarded as "inadmissible" until it is somehow corroborated. (One cannot, however, miss the clear double standard at play here in that these two authors demand that, in order to accept Allen's logbook as credible evidence, it be "scientifically tested to authenticate its date" but, at the same time, make no demands for such scientific tests to establish the authenticity of the actual quarry marks themselves or of Vyse's account of his "discovery" of them.)

So what is there, if anything, that could help corroborate or otherwise indicate the authenticity and veracity of Allen's logbook account? It seems that if Brewer did truly work with Vyse at the pyramids and did have a dispute with Raven and Hill about painting marks inside the pyramid and then charged them with forgery, this would surely have been enough to have Brewer's existence at Giza entirely expunged from Vyse's published work—*especially* so if there was any truth to such an allegation (a point that seems to have been entirely overlooked by Lawton and Ogilvie-Herald).

But even though Brewer's name is conspicuous by its absence in Vyse's *published* work, this may not be the case with Vyse's *private* journal. It occurred to me that if Brewer had, as Allen's account tells us, been working with Vyse and his team for some time before their dispute, then perhaps Brewer's name might be mentioned in Vyse's private journal but simply written out of his finished work, redacted from the official record of Vyse's operations for a rather obvious reason.

According to Allen's account, his great-grandfather had apparently ended up assisting Vyse at Giza only after his original mission with the British Medical Service to Egypt to assist in the design and construction of an eye infirmary for a Dr. Naylor (who was mentioned in Vyse's book) was cut short. It seems that Naylor's treatment for Egyptian workers with ophthalmia (a severe eye affliction) was unsuccessful, hence the reason why the hospital project did not go ahead. It seems that while Naylor returned to Europe, Brewer stayed on to assist Vyse and his team.

I tracked Vyse's private handwritten journal to a small library in Aylesbury, England, in April 2014, and later analysis of the six hundred or so pages (from digital photographs) showed that the journal did contain, at the relevant time period, what appeared to be the name Brewer and possibly even H. Brewer. It has to be stated, however, that Vyse's highly cursive handwritten style and the faintness of some of the ink make it difficult to be absolutely certain that the examples found are indeed the name Brewer.

Accepting, however, that Brewer was working with Vyse and his team at Giza in 1837, then we have to ask, Why would Vyse have totally expunged this name from his published work?

Skeptics such as Lawton and Ogilvie-Herald often point to the dispute between Vyse and Giovanni Caviglia, pointing out that Vyse writes extensively in his published work about the severe disagreement between these two men. (Caviglia had essentially accused Vyse of usurping the Italian explorer's discovery of the hidden stress-relieving chambers for himself, ensuring also that Caviglia was removed from the Giza site and that the firmaun was transferred to Vyse. It should be stated, however, in the interest of fairness, that Vyse rejected Caviglia's allegations and presented his own, quite different, account of the dispute.)[6] The reasoning goes that if Vyse could so openly write in his published book about the disagreement he had with Caviglia, then, had there also been a dispute with Brewer, Vyse would have had little problem also including that dispute in his published book. That Vyse made public the Caviglia dispute but not the Brewer dispute, the skeptics conclude, means there never was a dispute with anyone called Brewer, and by extension, Brewer didn't ever work for Vyse at Giza.

But this is a somewhat myopic view that serves merely to oversimplify the situation. While Caviglia was a very well-known, long-standing, and influential figure in Egypt with many important discoveries already to his name (and crucially with the search permit for Giza originally made in his name), Brewer, on the other hand, was but a young man barely twenty years of age, was fresh out of his studies to become a civil engineer, and had no standing or influence whatsoever with anyone in Egypt. He was the new kid on the block who had arrived on the scene almost by accident and, insofar as Vyse would have been concerned, of little significance. He most certainly would not have been, as Sitchin

Exhibit 3 • The Eyewitness   81

claimed and Lawton and Ogilvie-Herald repeated, one of Vyse's "senior staff."

Vyse's dispute with Caviglia was also a very public affair involving a number of other senior and influential people, and, as such, Vyse could hardly have avoided making mention of this dispute in his book to give his side of the story. However, the dispute with Brewer (assuming it did occur) would most certainly have been viewed by Vyse as an accusation from a "nonentity," a young upstart, and could have been easily handled internally, dismissed, and quietly brushed aside. And, naturally, after having made such an accusation against Vyse and his team, Brewer would undoubtedly have been regarded as persona non grata and immediately been given his marching orders from the site by the humorless Vyse—as seems to have been the case.

Other faults the skeptics find with Allen's brief account relate to the prize Brewer is said to have received for the design of a bridge over the Danube; they correctly point out that the only bridge being constructed across the Danube around Brewer's time was the Széchenyi Chain Bridge to link the cities of Buda and Pest, designed in 1839 by William Tierney Clark and completed by him in 1849. How then could Brewer possibly have received a prize for a bridge over the Danube when, clearly, it was Clark's bridge design that was built across this river? If this claim in Allen's account is so obviously wrong, the critics point out, then what else might be wrong?

The first thing to say here is that Brewer's obituary makes no mention of him having won such a prize for any such bridge, a rather glaring omission (were it to have been true), one would have thought. Notably, in Allen's logbook account it does not say that his great-grandfather's bridge design was actually built; all it states is that Brewer received a prize in Vienna (not Buda or Pest) for a design of a bridge to span the Danube.

This writer personally knows of architects and engineers today who have won prizes for designs of bridges to span the River Clyde in my home city of Glasgow—designs that were never actually built. And I also know that other bridges were subsequently built over the River Clyde having been designed by other designers. Winning a bridge design prize, perhaps at college or university, does not mean that your bridge design was ever intended to be built. And it does not say this in Allen's account—just that his great-grandfather won a prize for a bridge *design* in Vienna, and this may well be perfectly true.

It does seem, though, that Brewer did, in fact, spend some of his engineering career working on the Széchenyi Chain Bridge, for we are told in the *Watkins Express,* "The Engineer and General Superintendent of the Mines is Mr. Humphrey Brewer, who lives in a large white house on a knoll nearby. He is an Englishman by birth, and was an Assistant Engineer in the construction of a Suspension Bridge over the broad waters of the Danube. Drifting about he finally reached Blossburgh."[7]

But how would Brewer have come to work on this bridge? Brewer's father, William Jones Brewer, worked with engineer George Burge on Isambard Kingdom Brunel's Box Tunnel at Bath. Burge went on to win the contract for the foundations of the Széchenyi Chain Bridge; thus a loose connection with the Brewer family and this bridge is established via Burge.

It is perhaps the case, then, that later accounts of Brewer's life conflated these two quite separate events—his bridge design prize (perhaps won at university) and his later employment on the Széchenyi Chain Bridge—into one and the same event, thereby confusing later generations of Brewer's family into thinking their great-grandfather had designed the bridge that was eventually built across the Danube. Such are the perils of the oral tradition, but by the same token, this confusion, in a sense, actually adds credence to Allen's account; yes, it may be slightly muddled in places (like, for example, mistaking "Col." as an abbreviation for "Colin" Campbell as opposed to Colonel Patrick Campbell), but it was not at all the fabrication that some would have us believe. It would seem highly improbable that, if Allen's account were itself a hoax (as some skeptics have implied), it would include an episode in Brewer's life that could be so easily disproved.

TIME AND PLACE

Is there anything else that might help us determine the authenticity of Allen's logbook account? As it happens, this brief passage presents a

Exhibit 3 • The Eyewitness 83

couple of intriguing snippets that, on the balance of probability, point toward the account being a true and genuine record of historical events.

If we are to believe some of the skeptics who imply that Allen's account is but a fabrication, then whoever supposedly fabricated the account went out of their way to undertake extensive research into Allen's family history, even knowing fine details such as that Helen Pattengill (née Brewer) was known by the family as Aunt Nell; they knew which uncle was in the hospital in 1954 and knew the very house where Allen's mother was born.

Of course, some would argue that Allen himself knew all of this information and that he was party to Sitchin's (alleged) hoax and fabricated this account to help corroborate Sitchin's forgery theory. This is unlikely in the extreme, because there is other material contained in Allen's logbook account of the forgery at Giza that contradicts Sitchin's version as well as other information that neither Allen nor Sitchin could ever have known, information that has only come to light in 2014 as part of my own research into this controversy.

But there are other, much less obvious details that add credibility to Allen's logbook account. If this document was fabricated, then the research that went into producing it is truly remarkable. Certainly the names and roles of all the key players of Brewer's time at Giza (Campbell, Vyse, Naylor, Caviglia, Perring, Raven, and Hill) could have been easily gleaned from Vyse's published work (the most obvious source for information and one we know that Sitchin relied on heavily for his own research). But it is the subtle, almost inconsequential details in Allen's brief account that are far more revealing.

Allen writes in his notes that his great-grandfather traveled from "Bayruth to Athens" (presumably Beirut to Athens) and then onward through Austria and Prussia. Note that Allen writes "Prussia" and not Germany. Clearly we have someone here who understood that in 1837 Germany did not actually exist, so the use of the name Prussia in Allen's account is perfectly correct for the period.

But the depth of the historical understanding of this period goes much deeper. Given that there were no railway networks in 1837, how exactly would one have managed to travel from Athens directly to

Fig. 7.3. It is not currently possible to travel directly, by land or sea, from Athens into Austria, because Austria is a landlocked country bordered by many other countries.

Austria? Given that Austria is a landlocked country (fig. 7.3), it could not be reached by ship, so from Athens how would one have gotten there without passing through a number of other countries?

Brewer could easily have sailed from Beirut to Athens, but how could he then go from Athens directly to Austria? It is quite simple. In 1837, direct travel from Athens into Austria was perfectly feasible for, at that time, Austria was not the landlocked country that it is today but had an empire that extended all the way to the Adriatic Sea (fig. 7.4).

In other words, it would have been perfectly feasible for Brewer to travel by sea from Athens directly to Austria (probably to the seaport of Trieste, which is now part of northeast Italy) and from there onward through Austria and directly into Prussia—just as Allen's handed-down family account informs us. And it may well have been that on this homeward journey, possibly while sailing along the Danube, that

Exhibit 3 • The Eyewitness  85

Prussia
Austrian Empire

•Athens

Central Europe ca. 1837

*Fig.7.4. Austria in 1837 extended to the Adriatic Sea
and was bordered to the north by Prussia.*

Brewer learned of the bridge that was soon to be built across the river
(linking Buda and Pest) and used his father's connection to Burge to
gain employment there as an assistant engineer.

In another part of Allen's account, he writes:

> *Showed her [Allen's mother] in my log contact with Antarctic British
> Expedition but they didnt know who had arrived yet from England. It is
> spring down there.*[8]

This entry would seem to be a reference to a contact Allen had
made at that time (in 1954) with the British expedition to Antarctica,
presumably by shortwave radio communication. When we check the
Antarctic expedition records, we find that there was indeed a British-
Norwegian expedition to Antarctica in 1954 when Allen was writing
all of these events in his ham radio logbook. And one further small

detail here—Allen was based in Pittsburgh, Pennsylvania, and was writing this account in October 1954, which, of course, in Antarctica in the Southern Hemisphere would indeed have been the springtime; a small detail here for sure, but it is precisely this type of small detail that can so easily trip up the casual forger.

So, once again, we are confronted by an inordinate amount of remarkably detailed and accurate historical knowledge by the supposed fabricator of Allen's logbook. We are bound to ask, Is it likely that a supposed fabricator of this logbook account would have gone to such lengths, to offer such precise period detail and a deep understanding of the geopolitical state of the world in 1837, in order to produce a piece of fabricated evidence simply to back up a claim made by some author about the Great Pyramid? Or is it more likely that, invoking the principle of Occam's razor, the much simpler truth of the matter is that all these subtle historical details in Allen's account are accurate *not* as a result of extensive and detailed research on the part of some alleged hoaxer but simply because they are indeed part of a handed-down oral history from people who lived in and knew the world as it was in 1837?

THE WRONG NAME

There is one other telling detail to support that Allen's logbook page is not the result of research by some supposed fabricator. In Allen's account it seems that his great-grandfather Humphries Brewer had a dispute with both Raven and Hill about painted marks in the pyramid. Now, if Allen's logbook account was a fabrication (to support Sitchin's claim), then it stands to reason that Vyse's published book of his discoveries would have been the key source of information for any fabricator to understand the events and key players at Giza. As stated already, these books were certainly Sitchin's key source of information about Vyse's explorations.

However, in Vyse's *published* work he makes no mention anywhere in any of his volumes of Raven ever having assisted anyone, anywhere, at any time with the quarry marks that were supposedly found. According to Vyse's published account, Raven, along with a handful of others, was merely a witness to corroborate the likeness of the facsimile work

Exhibit 3 • The Eyewitness   87

undertaken by Hill (on Vyse's instruction). That witness attestation is the total extent of Raven's relationship to and involvement with the painted quarry marks in these chambers.

In his book Vyse informs us that he himself had copied some of the quarry marks, that he had instructed Hill to make 1:1 facsimiles of them, that Perring was to make a complete plan survey of the various chambers (including the quarry marks), and even that Mash had copied some hieroglyphs. But nowhere, not once in Vyse's entire published work, is Raven *ever* mentioned in the context of copying *any* of the quarry marks that were found.

In *Stairway to Heaven*, Sitchin, in making his initial allegation of forgery against Vyse, clearly understood this reality from Vyse's published account; that is, that Raven was simply *not* in the frame or in any way involved with painting any of the marks, and, as such, Sitchin implicates *only* Vyse, Hill, and (tacitly) Perring of having perpetrated forgery. He writes, "Were Vyse and Hill—possibly with the tacit connivance of Perring—morally capable of perpetrating such a forgery?"[9]

Sitchin clearly had no idea or even the remotest inkling that Raven was in any way involved, but Allen's 1954 logbook entry clearly indicates that he was. Thus, from a potential conspiracy point of view between Sitchin and Allen, it simply makes no sense whatsoever for Allen's account to accuse Raven of painting marks into the pyramid when there is no indication *anywhere* in Vyse's published work (Sitchin's primary source) of Raven ever having a paintbrush in his hand. It surely would have been better for a hoaxer (assuming, as some do, that the Allen logbook account was itself a fabrication) to have continued to identify the *same* people that Sitchin had already identified.

In summary then, Sitchin initially identifies Vyse, Hill, and (tacitly) Perring as the culprits, whereas Allen's account identifies Hill and Raven. If this were a conspiracy between Sitchin and Allen then surely the obvious course of action would have been to corroborate Sitchin's initial suspicions by identifying the *same culprits* (i.e., Vyse, Hill, and Perring) in Allen's account.

We will come back to this point in chapter 13 with another piece of evidence from Vyse's *private* journal, a piece of evidence that, contrary to Vyse's *published* account, does indeed place a paintbrush firmly in Raven's hand and, as such, corroborates Allen's logbook account, which states that Raven was indeed the accomplice to Hill, not, as Sitchin believed, Perring (although Perring may still have been tacitly involved).

THE PAINTED NAMES

Not all skeptics attempt to dismiss Allen's logbook out of hand, and some (even if begrudgingly) accept the authenticity of the account, if only at face value. They point out that the painting of marks that Raven and Hill were involved in within the Great Pyramid, as mentioned in Allen's logbook account, was nothing more than painting the names of Wellington, Nelson, Lady Arbuthnot, and Campbell into the chambers, as instructed by Vyse, who had dedicated specific chambers to each of those individuals.

Thus, the critics insist, the painting being done by Raven and Hill had nothing whatsoever to do with the forging of any hieratic quarry marks but was simply the innocent and "legitimate" painting of these names onto the stones in the newly discovered chambers.

Allen's logbook account, however, scotches this idea, as it clearly states, "Faint marks were repainted." The names of the British notables had only *just* been painted with heavy, black paint and would hardly have become "faint marks" that required repainting so soon. Thus Allen's account is clearly speaking of other faint marks that were repainted; that is, ancient marks that had faded with age, marks that required *red paint* and not the black paint used to dedicate the chambers to several illustrious British historical figures.

And why, in any case, would the names of Wellington and Nelson and so forth be described by Allen's great-grandfather as "marks"? The use of the word *marks* here is quite revealing and suggests unknown or unintelligible symbols (i.e., ancient hieratic quarry marks) having been repainted (and new ones painted). It is unlikely in the extreme that Brewer would have described the painting of any well-known British heroes' names as "some marks." These were obviously *names* Brewer would have been wholly familiar with, written in English he could read—not some obscure, unintelligible marks.

Exhibit 3 • The Eyewitness   89

And why, in any case, would Brewer have taken exception to the dedication of the chambers to Wellington and Nelson, the two heroes of Britain's wars against Napoleon? As an Englishman it is highly unlikely indeed that Brewer would have objected to the chambers being dedicated to two of Britain's national heroes, but one can certainly understand that a principled young man could very well have made a serious objection to placing *new* marks, *fake* hieratic marks inside the Great Pyramid, and he surely would have made his feelings on this known to Raven and Hill—and, it seems, to Vyse himself.

It rather seems that the simpler and more likely scenario here is that Raven and Hill used red ochre paint to repaint some marks (i.e., original quarry marks) that were "faint" but used the same red paint to place *new* marks (i.e., fake hieratic quarry marks such as gang names that included the king's various names, etc.) inside the relieving chambers. The implication is that at least *some* of the marks found within these chambers were indeed original marks, and, as we saw earlier in chapter 6, this is confirmed by some of Vyse's private journal entries where he states that when first entering Wellington's Chamber red-painted marks (that looked "nothing like hieroglyphics") were found on the east wall near the entrance.

The problem we have today is determining which marks are original and which were placed in the various chambers by Vyse and his team to perpetrate a hoax. At the end of the day, the mere fact of Vyse instructing names to be painted into various chambers brings *all* the painted marks into question. This is especially so given someone of the questionable moral character of Vyse being in charge of proceedings. This is to say that it cannot be denied that it remains entirely possible that the dispute between Brewer, Hill, and Raven concerned the painting of hieratic marks into the chambers as opposed to the names of Wellington, Nelson, and so forth, as some skeptics insist. And because that possibility cannot be discounted it must surely require us to revisit the entire question of these inscriptions, to perform tests, and to try to uncover scientific evidence to determine exactly what was done in these chambers by Vyse and his aides. We will consider such scientific evidence later in this book.

CHAPTER SEVEN SUMMARY

- It appears that there was a witness to Vyse's Great Pyramid fraud. In his book *Journeys to the Mythical Past,* Zecharia Sitchin presented a copy of a page from the radio logbook of Walter Allen from Pittsburgh, Pennsylvania. Allen wrote this entry into his logbook in 1954 while investigating his family's roots. He was told by some family elders that his great-grandfather Humphries Brewer worked with Vyse at Giza and that during his time there Brewer had a dispute with two of Vyse's assistants, Raven and Hill, about painted marks in the pyramid. Allen wrote in his logbook, "Faint marks were repainted, some were new."

- Critics, including authors Ian Lawton and Chris Ogilvie-Herald, question the authenticity of Allen's logbook account.

- In-depth analysis of the historical and geopolitical content of Allen's logbook entry suggests that the account is likely to be a genuine record of the events of 1837.

- Allen's account contradicts that of Sitchin, pointing the finger of blame at Vyse's assistants Henry Raven and J. R. Hill rather than Hill and John Shea Perring (as proposed by Zecharia Sitchin). This is highly peculiar, because there is no indication anywhere in Vyse's published account of Raven ever having drawn or painted any quarry marks; his input was seemingly limited only to witnessing (along with some others) some of the facsimile drawings made by Hill.

- It has been proposed that the painting being done by Raven and Hill was nothing more than the painting of names of people to whom Vyse had dedicated each of the chambers. This seems unlikely as these painted names could hardly have become faint so quickly that they required to be repainted. Nor is it likely that the names of British heroes such as Wellington and Nelson would be described by Allen's great-grandfather as "faint marks." The use of the word *marks* suggests unintelligible signs; that is, signs of hieratic script.

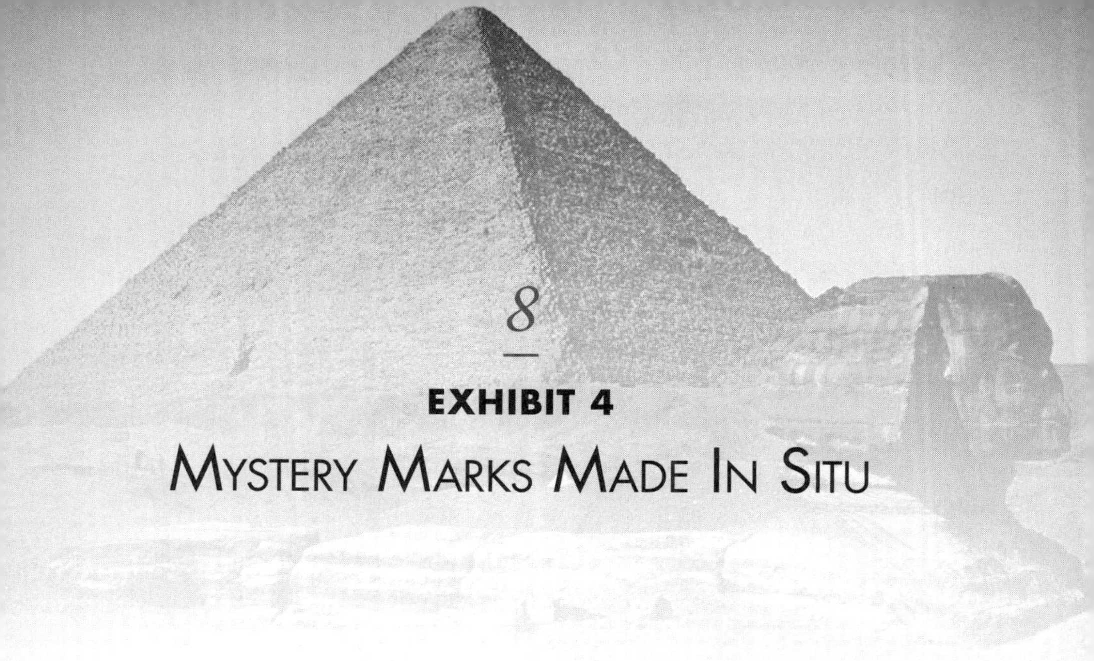

8

EXHIBIT 4
MYSTERY MARKS MADE IN SITU

As stated in previous chapters, Vyse and his team discovered and opened a series of four hitherto unknown chambers above Davison's Chamber within the Great Pyramid. All of these chambers were found to contain red-painted marks of some description, although some chambers had many more painted marks than others. The top two chambers opened by Vyse (Lady Arbuthnot's and Campbell's) had many more marks than the lower two chambers (Wellington's and Nelson's). The very lowest of these chambers, discovered some years earlier by Nathaniel Davison, has (thus far) failed to yield a single painted quarry mark.

One of the aspects of these marks we often find repeated in orthodox literature is that the quarry marks were placed on the blocks as they were being hewn out of the quarries and transported by the various work gangs—hence the name "quarry marks." This is why, we are told, the strings of script in the various chambers take on all manner of orientation, with some marks being perfectly upright (as viewed from a standing position in the chambers) and others entirely upside-down, while others are presented sideways (i.e., rotated 90° or 270°).

This somewhat jumbled array of marks is, of course, to be entirely expected, because the builders were not in the least concerned with properly presenting the gang names or other graffiti within the chambers; their priority was to place the blocks in the most convenient and efficient manner possible. Sometimes that would mean the marks would end up facing into the chambers, sometimes not. The overriding priority of the builders would also mean that, of those blocks with quarry marks that *did* end up facing into the chambers, these marks would take on whatever orientation was decided by the builders, whose main responsibility was simply finding the best means to place those particular blocks.

In essence then, it is the considered view of mainstream Egyptology that the quarry marks were painted onto the blocks some time before reaching the pyramid; few, if any, of the marks, it is believed, were actually painted onto the blocks after they were set in place within the pyramid. It is fair to say that if any of the marks had been painted onto in situ blocks (i.e., when the block was set in its final position at the pyramid), then those marks would, almost certainly, be presented upright (relative to an observer standing or crouching in the chamber) and would, most likely, have extended over one or more of the in situ blocks.

Work gang names painted onto the blocks at the quarries, however, would unlikely span more than one block (because these marks were each gang's specific identity denoting "ownership" of a particular block). As such, any hoaxer wishing to give the illusion that the block marks were genuine would have to make it appear that the marks were painted onto the blocks at the quarries and *not* in situ. Because any mark painted onto a block in situ would most likely be presented the correct way up, then by presenting the marks on the blocks with a jumble of orientations and making sure that none of the gang names spanned more than one block, an illusion is created that the marks were not painted in situ, ergo must have been painted onto the blocks *before* installation (at the quarries) and thus *must* be genuine. Thinking of this another way—if *all* these marks had been painted onto the roof and wall blocks with the same *right-way-up* orientation, then it becomes much easier to argue that the marks were painted in situ and *not* at the quarries, and, as such, it becomes much more difficult to assert an Old Kingdom provenance for them. This is to say that the jumbled orientations of the block marks could be nothing more than a clever but necessary ruse to convince the unwary observer that the block marks are authentic Old Kingdom graffiti.

Thus, what we find in the chambers is that strings of hieratic script are painted onto the blocks with various orientations and are con-

Exhibit 4 • Mystery Marks Made In Situ   93

fined to one block and one block only. Some of the marks, as might be expected, appear to be cut short or disappear behind a floor joint where the remainder of the marks cannot actually be observed. We will never know if such marks actually do continue behind these tight-fitting joints without knocking away a chunk of the stone—an intrusive and destructive process the Egyptian authorities are not ever likely to sanction. We simply have to take the Egyptologists at their word that the remainders of the partial marks that we can observe really do continue beyond the tight-fitting blocks.

MARKS MADE TO MEASURE

But there are some oddities to be observed here, peculiar anomalies in the presentation of the jumbled array of the painted marks found in these chambers; anomalies which may point to fraudulent activity.

In figure 8.1, we can immediately observe that the hieratic signs from Campbell's Chamber forming the quarry marks labeled "A" to "E" on the wall of this chamber are of different sizes. The signs that form quarry marks "A" are considerably smaller than those that form the marks labeled "C," which are themselves smaller than those signs labeled "D" and "E."

Upon closer inspection we observe that the available space between

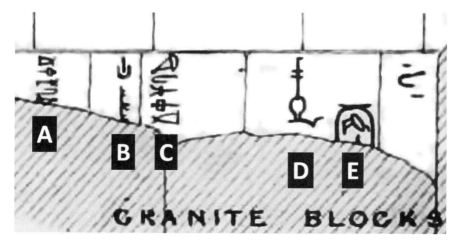

Fig. 8.1. Quarry marks in a section of Campbell's Chamber (north wall)

the granite floor blocks and the top of each wall block is also different for marks labeled "A" to "E." Here we see that the available gap for the quarry marks on the wall block (at position "A") is considerably less than the gaps available for the marks labeled "C," "D," and "E." In other words, the characters written into gap "A" have to be smaller than those written into gaps "C" to "E" simply because there is much less available space in gap "A" for the painter of these marks to work with.

This sizing of the signs to neatly fit into the available gap between the floor block and the top of the wall block appears indicative of someone who has written these marks in situ, ensuring that the characters labeled "A" fit snugly into the available gap, and when given a slightly bigger gap to work with (i.e., at "C," "D," and "E"), the glyphs become ever more expansive to better utilize the greater space.

MISSING PARTS

If we now consider the glyphs in figure 8.1 "C," we can see that these make up the partial gang name "The gang, the White Crown of Khnum-Khuf is powerful." However, the cartouche element of this gang name is not present on this block, and, in consideration of the ancient Egyptian writing convention known as "honorific transposition," the only positions the cartouche could be presented on this block are either immediately above or immediately to the left of this partial gang name (as observed). Given that this block would have been cut to this specific height at the quarry (in order to accomodate the inclined roof block directly above), then there is simply no space above the existing text ("C") to place the cartouche. Nor is it likely that the block would have been cut shorter at the side (thus removing the cartouche element). This is to say that whoever painted this part of the gang name onto this block did so in such a way as to make it *impossible* to properly position the cartouche element of this gang name. In short, it appears that this partial gang name has been painted onto this block by someone who was entirely unfamiliar with the ancient Egyptian rule of honorific transposition.

It is possible, however, that the obscure marks labeled "B" (fig. 8.1) may be the remnant of the missing cartouche from this partial gang

Exhibit 4 • Mystery Marks Made In Situ 95

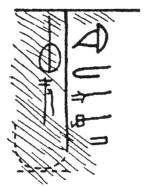

Fig. 8.2. The missing cartouche of the partial gang name labeled "C" may be to the left as indicated by the dotted outline. (Image: Alan Rowe)

name, and this is certainly suggested by the drawing of Egyptologist Alan Rowe (fig. 8.2).[1]

However, given Perring's plan survey drawing of this section of wall in Campbell's Chamber then the possible cartouche element of this gang name (as presented by Rowe) has been painted onto a *separate adjacent wall block,* and, as such, we then have an example—the *only* example—of a gang name that has been written across *two* adjacent wall blocks and thus presents a clear sign of fakery, because the quarry gangs would simply *never* have done this; they would have placed their full gang name on *both* of the individual stone blocks they had quarried. Indeed, that the possible cartouche element here is so obscure may, in fact, be the result of the forger realizing this mistake and attempting to "correct" it by erasing the cartouche element on the second block, ensuring it was unrecognizable. But the positioning of the partial gang name (fig. 8.1 "C") fails to take into account ancient Egyptian writing convention and, as such, exposes this attempt at deception.

A similar situation arises with the quarry marks labeled "E" (fig. 8.1). This partial Khufu cartouche is part of the gang name "The gang, Companions of Khufu." Given the particular orientation of these marks and in consideration of ancient Egyptian writing convention, then the remainder of this gang name—given its clear absence from *above* the partial cartouche—can *only* be placed to the left of the partial cartouche (as per fig. 8.1 "D"). However, the marks labeled "D" in Perring's plan drawing do not show any other signs that are clearly identifiable as belonging to this particular gang name; a rather glaring omission.

Fig. 8.3. One of the missing gang name signs is presented below the partial cartouche. (Image: Alan Rowe)

It should be said, however, that another drawing by Rowe of this partial cartouche, labeled "E" in figure 8.1, *does* present what *may* be one of the missing gang name signs (the *apr* determinative sign for "gang")[2] to the left of (i.e., below) the partial Khufu cartouche (fig. 8.3).

However, without an actual photograph of these particular marks, it is impossible to be certain as to who has made the most accurate drawing of them—Perring or Rowe?

NOT SO IMPOSSIBLE MARKS

It has been noted by a number of researchers over the years that a number of quarry marks can be observed between the immovable blocks of these chambers where the gap between the blocks is so narrow (about one inch or so) that no fraudster could possibly ever get a brush into let alone draw anything meaningful. This fact is held up by Egyptologists to assert the authenticity of *all* the painted marks in these chambers (ignoring the obvious fact that all of the king's names are painted onto blocks in easily accessible places). Indeed, as a result of this realization, international bestselling author Graham Hancock, having been permitted by Zahi Hawass to examine the painted marks in these chambers, issued the following position statement.

> I have changed my views on the validity of the forgery theory [of Sitchin]. The relieving chambers are strictly off-limits to the public and are extremely difficult to gain access to. I had been unable to obtain permission to visit them prior to the publication of *Keeper/ Message* in 1996. However in December 1997, Zahi Hawass allowed

Exhibit 4 • Mystery Marks Made In Situ 97

me to spend an entire day exploring these chambers. There were no restrictions on where I looked, and I had ample time to examine the hieroglyphs closely, under powerful lights. Cracks in some of the joints reveal hieroglyphs set far back into the masonry. No "forger" could possibly have reached in there after the blocks had been set in place—blocks, I should add, that weigh tens of tons each and that are immovably interlinked with one another. The only reasonable conclusion is the one which orthodox Egyptologists have already long held—namely that the hieroglyphs are genuine Old Kingdom graffiti and that they were daubed on the blocks before construction began.[3]

This position statement was followed in 2011 by the following qualified retraction.

In *Fingerprints* I supported the Vyse forgery theory. Later when I got into the relieving chambers myself and saw that some quarry marks disappear far back into the gaps between the blocks I felt that I must be wrong to support the forgery theory—because no one could have gotten a brush into those gaps to carry out the forgery. Therefore the quarry marks must be genuine and must have been put on the blocks before they were put into place in the chamber. Accordingly I retracted the position I had taken in *Fingerprints*.

It's possible I threw the baby out with the bathwater with that retraction. Unlike the unforgeable quarry marks positioned between the blocks, the Khufu cartouche is in plain view and could easily have been forged by Vyse.

I do not insist it was, I just accept that it could have been, and that some interesting doubts have been raised over its authenticity. I await further evidence one way or the other.[4]

In a subsequent communication with Hancock, I presented him (in a private e-mail) with the following question: "When you say there are 'quarry marks' in the tight gaps between the blocks, are you meaning these are 'mason's markings' or are they actual hieroglyphic markings? If, hieroglyphs, are you aware if any of them say 'Khufu'"?

Hancock responded to my question as follows: "It's a long time ago now, but I [am] 100 per cent certain that none say 'Khufu.' Nor are they lines/registers of hieroglyphs. They are simple, isolated and (though I am no expert in these things) look like typical quarry marks to me."

Hancock concedes that he is "no expert" in such matters but that the markings in these tight gaps between the blocks, in his experience, appeared more like "typical quarry marks," and there were no cartouches that he could see in any of the cracks between the blocks. This, of course, needs to be confirmed, but it appears to be the case that the full and partial Suphis/Khufu cartouches inscribed in Campbell's Chamber appear only in open and easily accessible places—the partial example on a wall block and the complete example on a roof block.

But even if it transpires that there is some Old Kingdom hieratic script (rather than mason's building symbols or some other unrecognizable marks) in the tight gaps between the immovable blocks in these chambers, it remains entirely possible that even these marks in such inaccessible places could still have been forged; yes, there is indeed a means by which even this seemingly impossible feat could have been achieved—and relatively easily too.

Independent pyramid researcher Dennis Payne informs us that what is required in this instance is not any kind of painter's brush but rather some string and two sheets of stiff card or thin board. The string (forming the shapes of the required quarry marks) is fixed with an adhesive to one of the thin boards and is then painted over with red ochre paint (which was still being made and was available in 1837). This board with its freshly painted string signs (i.e., hieratic quarry marks) is slid into the narrow gap between two adjacent blocks. Having done this, a second thin board is then slid in behind the first board, thus jamming and impressing the painted string "quarry marks" from the first board onto the face of the stone block within the tight gap. This impression having been completed, the second board is then removed, followed by the first board. The fake quarry marks are now presented deep within a seemingly impossible place—a tight gap between immovable blocks where no forger could possibly get a paintbrush. So, once again, what was once held by Egyptologists to be an impossible task is shown to be not so impossible after all.

Exhibit 4 • Mystery Marks Made In Situ 99

MARKS PAINTED IN SITU

But if these marks were indeed painted in situ, as a close analysis of the available evidence seems to suggest, then how likely is it that an ancient Egyptian scribe, standing on the granite floor of the chamber with the wall or roof block in front of him, would have squeezed these marks sideways (or upside-down) into tight gaps on single stone blocks when, theoretically, the entire horizontal block or even the entire chamber wall would have been available to him on which to daub his graffiti?

Or is the simpler answer to this conundrum that someone else painted these marks sideways onto these blocks simply to make it *appear* as though they had *not* been written in situ, ergo they must have been painted at the quarries; that is, before the blocks were set in place, ergo we are obliged to conclude that they must be genuine Old Kingdom marks? This may indeed be what the forger wishes us to believe from the haphazard arrangement of these painted marks, but the telltale clues that these marks were painted in situ are there for anyone to see.

Take this other example, this time from Lady Arbuthnot's Chamber (fig. 8.4). Notice how the lower set of characters (image 2) follows the

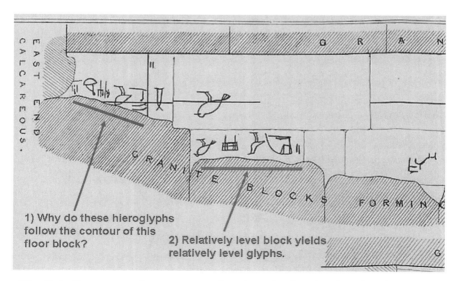

Fig. 8.4. Quarry marks in section of Lady Arbuthnot's Chamber (east wall)

contours of a relatively level granite floor block, and note also how these marks fit perfectly into the available space between the top of the wall block and the granite floor block. Now consider the upper set of characters (image 1); notice how these characters follow the contour of the sloping granite floor block.

Once again we are confronted with evidence of quarry marks that appear to have been painted onto blocks in situ. And we have to ask again, If these were indeed painted in situ, as seems to be the case, then why on earth would the painter, standing on the granite floor of the chamber, paint these marks upside-down or sideways onto a single block when he would have had the entire wall of the chamber on which to paint the marks the correct way up?

Our final example again comes from Lady Arbuthnot's Chamber (fig. 8.5). Notice how the quarry marks indicated by the arrows appear to follow the contours of the granite floor blocks. Once again we observe what appears to be evidence of marks that have been written in situ, and once again, if that is the case, we have to ask, Why would an ancient Egyptian scribe paint these marks on the wall upside-down (or sideways), and why would he constrain each set of marks to a single block?

And why, we must also ask, are there just a handful of inscriptions

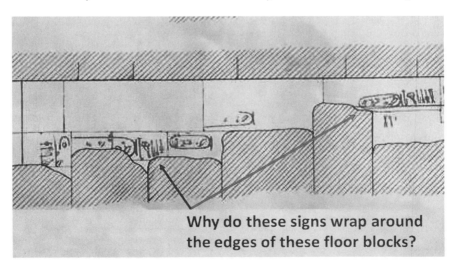

Why do these signs wrap around the edges of these floor blocks?

Fig. 8.5. Quarry marks in section of Lady Arbuthnot's Chamber (north wall)

Exhibit 4 • Mystery Marks Made In Situ 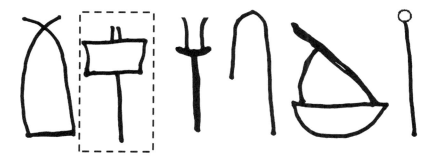 101

that are oriented upright (relative to a standing position)? A quick analysis of the stones in the various chambers shows that, of some forty stone blocks (each with four possible orientations), only three blocks present marks with an upright orientation when, from a purely statistical perspective, one might reasonably have expected 25 percent (ten blocks or thereabouts) to present upright marks. Why are the vast majority of the painted marks on these stones set at 90°, 180° or 270°? Has someone been overegging the pudding, trying too hard to make a convincing illusion?

In whatever chamber we care to scrutinize, we are confronted time and time again by a number of anomalies that present significant contradictions and challenges to the conventional narrative of the marks found in these chambers as related to us from the account of Vyse. The simplest explanation for this may be that the marks were oriented in this haphazard manner to make it *appear* as though they were painted onto the blocks at the quarries, with the implication, thereof, that they must be genuine marks. We will revisit this question of blocks being painted in situ in chapters 9 and 11, with some further, more damning evidence.

A MYSTERY SIGN

Within the chambers opened by Vyse and his team, a specific series of hieratic signs were said to have been found (fig. 8.6). Ann Macy Roth

Fig. 8.6. This series of hieroglyphs reads "The gang, the White Crown [of Khnum-Khuf] is powerful." The sign in the dashed box is not fully understood by Egyptologists and, to this day, remains something of a mystery.

and others believe a mystery sign in this series (highlighted in the dashed box, fig. 8.6) may be an early hieratic sign for the sail hieroglyph. However, given that the ancient Egyptian sail glyph had not evolved into a hieratic form that sufficiently (though not exactly) resembled this mystery sign until much later in the Old Kingdom[5] (hundreds of years after the Great Pyramid was built and the upper relieving chambers sealed), other Egyptologists contend that this mystery sign cannot be the sail glyph, and some consider that it may, instead, be a poorly rendered hand-drill sign (fig. 8.7).

Of course, if Egyptologists are correct in their belief that this mystery sign is but a poorly rendered drill sign, then the obvious question arises as to why the painter of this sign failed to write it correctly on the blocks at the quarries. After all, one must assume that the ancient Egyptian scribe responsible for marking the quarried blocks with the appropriate gang name would at least have known how to write the name properly, even if crudely with red ochre paint.

Why then has this sign in this gang name been so poorly rendered (i.e., the bottom part of the drill sign is entirely missing), and more to the point, why has this "mistake" been replicated on no less than *eight* different occasions within the relieving chambers?

It is perhaps understandable that the drill sign on the occasional

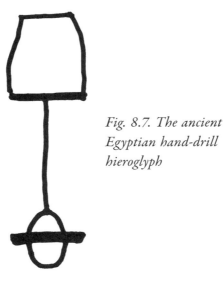

Fig. 8.7. The ancient Egyptian hand-drill hieroglyph

Exhibit 4 • Mystery Marks Made In Situ   103

block here or there might have been scuffed and damaged in transport, thereby losing the bottom part of the sign, but is it reasonable to suspect that such a thing occurred on *eight* different occasions, lobbing off the same bottom part of the drill glyph each and every time? And we also have to ask: Is it reasonable to expect that an ancient Egyptian scribe would repeat such a mistake eight times? Is this really the work of an ancient Egyptian scribe, who would surely have understood how to write his own language?

It is, of course, entirely possible that Egyptologists have not, as yet, correctly identified this particular sign and that it is not, as some believe, a poorly rendered drill (or sail) sign at all but some other sign altogether. As yet, however, Egyptology remains divided on other possibilities for this sign. But there is another possibility that might explain this anomaly, one that is entirely consistent with the evidence.

Might this disputed sign in this gang name perhaps be the work of someone else, someone much more recent who had very little knowledge of ancient Egyptian writing, who perhaps found *one* poorly preserved version of this gang name and, in his ignorance, assumed the sign had been correctly drawn by the original ancient Egyptian scribe, then simply replicated the sign, fault and all, eight times throughout these chambers? If the mystery sign never actually existed as a sign in its own right in ancient Egypt but came about only through a fraudster's "mistake," might this perhaps explain why modern Egyptologists struggle to definitively identify this sign? And, of course, it stands to reason that if this sign (and gang name) has been faked eight times in these chambers, then any accompanying cartouche of Khnum-Khuf from this gang name is most likely to have also been faked.

CHAPTER EIGHT SUMMARY

- Because of the jumbled arrangement of signs on the blocks within the various relieving chambers of the Great Pyramid, it is the view of mainstream Egyptology that the signs were painted outside the chambers; that is, at the stone quarries (hence the name "quarry marks").

- In Campbell's Chamber strings of signs have been painted onto the blocks and sized appropriately to fit precisely into the available space between the granite floor and the top of the wall blocks. As the available space between the floor block and the top of the wall block increased, the additional space was utilized to paint larger signs. This is indicative of in-situ painting.

- In Lady Arbuthnot's Chamber signs can be observed on the east and north walls, following the contours of the granite floor blocks, thereby indicating in-situ painting.

- It is unlikely that authentic in-situ marks would have been restricted to a single block or that they would have been painted with any orientation other than upright. That the quarry marks have been presented in a jumbled manner may have been contrived to convince the casual observer that the marks had been painted outside the chamber—that is, at the quarries—and, as such, that they must therefore be contemporary with the pyramid.

- Statistically speaking, we should expect to see many more blocks with signs with an upright orientation than are actually present throughout the various chambers.

- A sign within the White Crown gang name, believed by some Egyptologists to be a sail or drill, has been drawn incorrectly no less than *eight* times throughout the chambers. It seems unlikely that an ancient Egyptian scribe would draw a sign incorrectly eight times. More likely is that one badly preserved or scuffed sign has been copied eight times, thus replicating the "misprint" throughout the chambers and may explain why Egyptologists struggle to definitively identify this mystery sign.

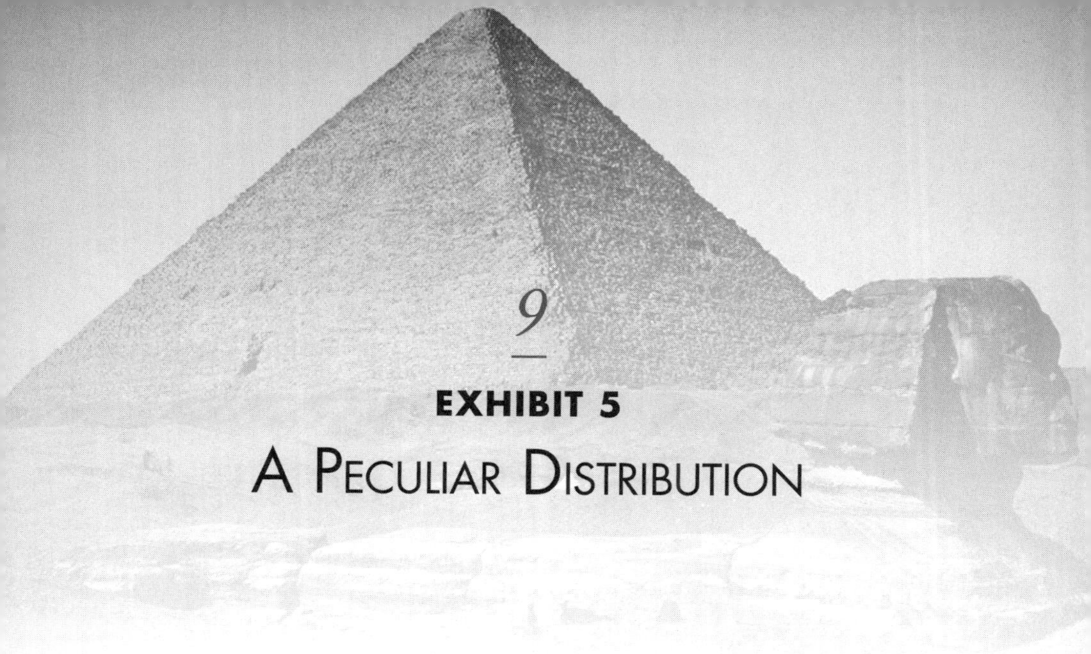

9

EXHIBIT 5

A PECULIAR DISTRIBUTION

In the previous chapter we learned that the distribution of the painted marks throughout the various upper chambers of the Great Pyramid seemed a somewhat haphazard affair, noting that not a single quarry mark has ever been discovered by anyone in Davison's Chamber, the lowest of the relieving chambers; a few marks were found in the next two chambers, Wellington's and Nelson's; while the final two chambers, Lady Arbuthnot's and Campbell's, presented, by some considerable way, the most painted marks.

If we now consider the theory of Ann Macy Roth, we realize that this is a most unusual situation indeed. This is, Roth proposes, because specific work gangs were responsible for the construction of particular sides of the pyramid and, by extension, specific walls of the internal chambers, including Davison's Chamber and the four chambers blasted open by Vyse. Simplistically speaking, Roth suggests that the builders' gang names would be confined to specific walls (mainly the north and south wall but also, to a lesser extent, the east and west wall) and that these gang names would only ever be found at the cardinal direction for which a particular gang was responsible for constructing. Roth further suggests that this system of working would essentially be the same and hold true for the walls of the Great Pyramid's internal relieving chambers; specific gang names (along with their particular version of the king's name) would only ever be associated with a

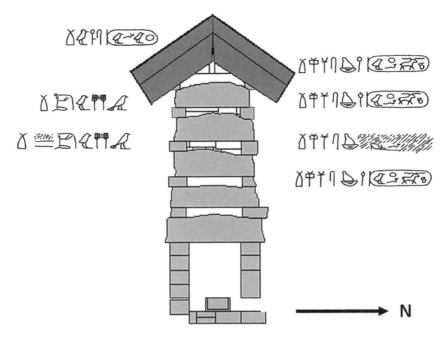

Fig. 9.1. Distribution of gang names in relieving chambers of the Great Pyramid (Image: Scott Creighton, based on original drawing by Ann Macy Roth)

particular side of the pyramid and the walls of its internal chambers.

In her book *Egyptian Phyles in the Old Kingdom: The Evolution of a System of Social Organization,* Roth presents a diagram similar to the one in figure 9.1. As can be seen from Roth's distribution there are no marks at all in the lowest chamber (Davison's). It seems from her chart that all the northern walls of the relieving chambers (except Davison's) are somewhere inscribed with the same gang name, "The gang, the White Crown of Khnum-Khuf is powerful." The southern walls, by contrast, are inscribed only in the top three chambers, but with two different gang names.

Roth explains:

> In the following reign of Khufu, the gang seems to have been the most important unit of organization. The texts inscribed on the side

Exhibit 5 • A Peculiar Distribution 107

walls of the relieving chambers of the Great Pyramid name three gangs, each based on a different form of the king's name. Seven blocks give a gang name based on his Horus name, *Hr-Mddw* [Hor Medjedu]; ten give a name based on the full form of his *nswt-bjtj* name, Khnum-Khufu; and two blocks give a name based on the abbreviated form of that name, Khufu. . . .

The distribution of the gang names on the walls of the relieving chambers is an interesting foreshadowing of later developments. In each chamber the blocks of the north side are marked with one gang name and those of the south side with another, while the end walls [west and east] are divided in half and the blocks are marked with the name of the gang whose name is on the nearest side wall.[1]

From a cursory examination of Roth's diagram and her commentary that goes with it, it would seem to be the case that this practice was employed in the construction of the Great Pyramid and its internal chambers. And it follows that if this were indeed the case, then it is unlikely that Vyse or his assistants would have been aware of such a practice in order to replicate it—so the orthodox argument goes. Thus, it is inferred, the painted marks in these chambers must therefore be genuine.

However, if we dig a little deeper into Roth's hypothesis with specific regard to the gang names on the various walls of these chambers, things do not appear to be as neat and certain as her diagram suggests. The first thing to say here is that by simple statistical probability we should expect to have found some similar marks in the lowest chamber (Davison's). Also, we should expect to find a similar frequency of marks; this is to say that we should expect to find a more even distribution of the various gang names throughout the chambers. But we simply don't find any of this. What we find in reality is this:

1. Davison's Chamber: No marks of any kind on any of the walls.
2. Wellington's Chamber: Gang name (White Crown gang) on the west wall only. Partial Khnum-Khuf cartouche (presumably also of the White Crown gang) on the east wall.

3. Nelson's Chamber: Two different gang names (White Crown gang and Pure Ones of the Hor Medjedu gang), both on the west wall only.

4. Lady Arbuthnot's Chamber: Two different gang names (White Crown gang and Pure Ones of the Hor Medjedu gang) on the south wall. Two different gang names on the west wall (Pure Ones of the Hor Medjedu gang and the White Crown gang). Five occurrences of the same gang name (White Crown gang) on the north wall.

5. Campbell's Chamber: Two occurrences of the same gang name (Friends/Companions of Khufu) on the south roof gable. Two occurrences of the same gang name (White Crown gang) on the north wall.

Some other points to note relating to the distribution of these gang names include:

1. Other than some peculiar marks on the east wall of Wellington's Chamber (mentioned in chapter 6) and with the exception of a couple of small partial markings on the east wall of Campbell's Chamber, there are no marks of any kind on the east wall of any other chamber and certainly no gang names.

2. Almost twice as many of these chamber walls are without gang names as those with gang names.

3. Most gang names are concentrated in Lady Arbuthnot's chamber.

4. Across all the relieving chambers, the south walls bear three different gang names.

5. Two chambers (Nelson's and Lady Arbuthnot's) have two different gang names on the same cardinal side.

6. Campbell's chamber may have a partial Friends/Companions of Khufu gang name on the north wall along with the White Crown gang name.

7. Across all the chambers, the White Crown gang name (full or partial) is found on a wall in every cardinal direction: a

Exhibit 5 • A Peculiar Distribution 109

north wall (Campbell's); a north, south, and west wall (Lady Arbuthnot's); and an east and west wall (Wellington's).

In support of her theory, Roth cites the distribution of some gang names found upon stones of the mortuary temple complex of Menkaure as supporting evidence of this theorized practice. But it has to be said, if Roth was able to make such an observation at Menkaure's mortuary temple and come to such a conclusion, then surely Vyse, who also excavated this complex during his Giza operations, could have noticed it as well and made note of this distribution and simply replicated the (theorized) practice within the Great Pyramid's upper chambers.

But, as shown above, it is highly doubtful that such a practice even existed, because, far from being the relatively straightforward, neat distribution Roth's diagram suggests, if anything, the distribution pattern of the gang names we find within the relieving chambers is so apparently random that it appears to be the work of someone who clearly didn't know of, or understand, this theorized practice of ancient Egyptian pyramid building.

FURTHER DISTRIBUTION ANOMALIES

Photographic images of the various relieving chambers are very few and far between, with the vast bulk of images in the public domain having come from Campbell's Chamber, which bears the famous Khufu cartouche. However, recent television documentaries have appeared featuring the likes of Zahi Hawass in the other lower chambers, discussing their features with archaeological students and TV reporters. What has become apparent from these documentaries is the fact that the walls of the lower chambers (mainly Wellington's and Nelson's) are caked in lime slurry, the once-liquid mixture seen running down the various walls of these chambers. This spillage down the face of the wall blocks would have occurred when the builders were sliding the roofing blocks of the chambers into place, using the slurry (a mixture of lime and water) as a lubricant to help reduce friction between the blocks.

The curious thing to observe here is that in those chambers where the most lime slurry is observed on the walls (Wellington's and Nelson's), we find the fewest painted marks, and in those chambers that present the least amount of wall slurry (Lady Arbuthnot's and Campbell's), we find the most painted marks inscribed on the walls. And stranger still, we find that there is not a single report—historical or otherwise—that notes any quarry marks (or even partial quarry marks) under this wall slurry. This is particularly odd as we have reports from the pioneering Egyptologist Sir William Flinders Petrie of black-and-red leveling lines drawn by the masons on these walls that apparently go under and over the wall slurry, but, strangely, the painted "quarry marks" all manage to avoid being covered by any of these long runnels of wall slurry. If these marks were truly painted onto these blocks at the quarries, then, surely, we should observe at least some marks, or even partial marks, peeking out from beneath the long runnels of slurry that can be observed running down the walls in these chambers.

It almost seems as though someone has deliberately avoided presenting any quarry marks on the walls where there is a lot of slurry and concentrated his effort on those walls where there is much less slurry (e.g., Lady Arbuthnot's Chamber). If these painted marks truly are genuine then this is a very unnatural state of affairs and a distribution that we would not normally expect to find. However, from the perspective of a hoax then such a peculiar distribution becomes perfectly understandable.

If a forger wished to make these marks appear original (i.e., that they were painted onto the blocks at the quarries), then painting the marks on top of the dried slurry would serve only to undermine such a deception, because it would then be abundantly clear that the marks could only have been placed onto the blocks in situ (i.e., after the slurry had dried). So from a potential forger's point of view, painting glyphs on top of the dried slurry would have had to be avoided at all costs.

Another observation that also seems to run contrary to Roth's hypothesis is the fact that we find that not a single quarry mark has been reported to have been found on any of the granite *ceiling* or *floor* blocks of these chambers—a most curious situation as these blocks present two observable faces (the topside and underside) instead of one

Exhibit 5 • A Peculiar Distribution 🦅 111

observable surface like the wall and inclined roof blocks present. The quarry workers at the Giza and Tura quarries apparently placed quarry marks on their quarried blocks, but it seems that only the quarry workers much farther away at Aswan, where the granite blocks of Campbell's Chamber were quarried, did not do likewise.

Of course, from a potential forger's point of view, this makes perfect sense even if, ultimately, it presents a glaring anomaly. As stated previously, the key objective of the forger is to make the marks appear genuine. To do this the forger paints many of these marks onto the wall blocks sideways or upside-down. Because it is reasonable to assume that anyone sitting within the chamber painting marks onto the blocks in situ would have drawn them the right way up, it then follows that finding the marks in a variety of orientations naturally suggests that the marks were placed onto the blocks at the quarry (right way up), but by the time the blocks reached the pyramid they had been turned to different orientations to best fit them into place within the structure. Thus, if it is logically deduced that the marks were painted onto the block at the quarry, then, logically, they must surely be genuine Old Kingdom hieratic markings. So the orthodox reasoning goes. It is the haphazard orientations of the wall marks that enable the Egyptologists to logically deduce such a conclusion.

By contrast, however, the accessible surfaces of ceiling or floor blocks present flat planes—they have cardinal directions but have no up or down, and, as such, it is not possible to have any marks on the underside (ceiling) or topside (floor) in an upright or upside-down manner, and, as such, no logical conclusion about the provenance could be deduced from marks on such flat surfaces. It is perhaps for this reason that any forger naturally would have concentrated on placing his fake marks on the chamber's vertical walls and inclined roof blocks, for only these planes permit us to determine orientation (relative to the chamber) and to then make a deduction about their provenance (i.e., that the marks were made not in situ but at the quarries). But neglecting to place at least some marks on the surfaces of the ceiling or floor blocks serves only to undermine the overall effect, for surely if this was a normal practice of the quarry gangs of this period then we should expect to have found at least some marks, partial or otherwise, on the two visible surfaces of these granite ceiling/floor blocks.

CHAPTER NINE SUMMARY

- It is theorized that specific gangs were responsible for the construction of specific sides of the pyramids and also their internal chambers. As such it is theorized that gang names would be confined to particular chamber walls and only those walls. It is asserted that any forger in 1837 would have been totally unaware of such a theorized practice in order to replicate it.
- A close analysis of the distribution of quarry gang names throughout the various upper pyramid chambers does not appear to support this theory; the gang name distribution, rather than conforming to such a theorized practice, appears much more random and haphazard.
- Chambers with the greatest amount of visible lime slurry on the walls present the fewest number of painted marks, while the chambers with the least amount of visible slurry present the most painted marks on the walls.
- While red and black painted mason's leveling lines are seen to run under and over wall slurry, there are no reports of any quarry marks, partial or otherwise, under the runnels of lime slurry.
- While many painted marks have been found on the chamber walls and gabled roof blocks (from the Giza and Tura quarries), no reports have been made of any "quarry marks" having been found on any of the numerous granite floor/ceiling blocks from the more distant Aswan quarries.

10

EXHIBIT 6

THE LIE OF THE LANDSCAPES

Our next piece of evidence comes from something that is so obvious that no one actually notices it, or if they do, they consider it to be of little relevance. It may seem like a fastidious point to raise, but the orientation of all three instances of the Khufu cartouche copied from Campbell's Chamber that we find in Vyse's private journal are, oddly, oriented *horizontally*. Why should this be when the actual gang name with its Khufu cartouche (fig. 1.9, p. 9) is painted *vertically/sideways* onto the inclined roof block (i.e., top-to-bottom with the signs rotated at 90° to Vyse's drawings of them in his private journal)? Why didn't Vyse draw the cartouche from this gang name in his private field notes exactly as he would have seen it on the roof block, maintaining its vertical/sideways orientation?

It may seem a trivial point, but when we consider all the other hieroglyphic and hieratic drawings in Vyse's journal, we find that all these other signs are drawn exactly and correctly as he would have observed them: sometimes upright, sometimes upside-down (i.e., rotated 180°), and sometimes sideways (i.e., rotated 90° or 270°). With his body as the frame of reference (i.e., head to top of chamber, feet to bottom of chamber), all these other drawings in his private journal present us with evidence of how Vyse *instinctively* would have drawn the glyphs he observed in the chambers, giving each drawing the correct orientation relative to the axis of his body; in short, Vyse drew in his journal exactly what was in front of him, maintaining the particular orientation of the hieroglyphic and hieratic signs as he stood and copied them.

This practice of maintaining the orientation of a particular piece of text would have been all the more essential as many of the signs we find today in the chambers and drawn by Vyse in his private journal were quite abstract in form, and without considerable knowledge of hieratic script, it would have been impossible for Vyse to know which way up a particular abstract sign should be. As such, it would have been absolutely vital for Vyse to draw the signs exactly as he saw them, capturing the given orientation, which would better enable the experts back in London to determine the true orientation and meaning of the various marks. This is to say that a particular group of abstract signs could potentially be mistranslated if the given orientation of the signs was not properly and consistently recorded. And, of course, it was not Vyse's job to interpret any of the signs, merely to accurately copy them.

We surely have to ask then, given the *other* examples of glyphs in his private journal where the orientation of the marks as they actually appear in the various chambers is maintained, Why then did Vyse decide to draw in his private diary on *three* occasions the Khufu cartouche (ostensibly from Campbell's Chamber) rotated some 90° from how this cartouche actually appears? Are we perhaps detecting a clue as to how Vyse *originally* observed the Khufu cartouche and, therefore, why it takes a left-to-right orientation with all the signs drawn perfectly upright in his written journal? Did Vyse originally copy a Khufu cartouche that had been *horizontally* aligned from some other place? Did Vyse have Raven and Hill copy into Campbell's Chamber a horizontally aligned Suphis/Khufu cartouche that had been found *elsewhere* outside the Great Pyramid and, without fully thinking through the ramifications of the next decision, simply rotated the original horizontal cartouche by 90°; that is placing what had originally been a horizontally aligned cartouche (copied from somewhere outside the pyramid) vertically into the chamber, thereby creating the contradiction with his three horizontal journal entries?

Admittedly, this particular line of questioning may seem somewhat pedantic, but, remarkably, we find that it is a behavioral pattern that is emulated in the facsimile drawings of Vyse's assistant J. R. Hill, and to a quite remarkable degree.

Exhibit 6 • The Lie of the Landscapes 115

HILL'S ORIENTATIONS

During some unrelated research in 2013, I had been sent copies of three of Hill's facsimile drawings by Patricia Usick, Ph.D., of the British Museum. In studying these drawings I felt there was something odd about them, but at the time I couldn't quite put my finger on what it was. I subsequently contacted Usick again in April 2014, asking if she could send me scanned copies of Hill's other facsimile drawings (twenty-eight in all) so that I could examine them in order to perhaps figure out what it was that was nagging my mind. Unfortunately, Usick explained to me that there were no digital scans or photos of the other Hill facsimiles that she could send. The only way I would be able to examine them would be to arrange an appointment with her, which I duly did.

So, on a beautiful spring day in May 2014, my wife, Louise, and I set off from our home in Glasgow, Scotland, for the British Museum (fig. 10.1), a round trip of a thousand miles or so. We didn't know it

Fig. 10.1. The British Museum (Image: Scott Creighton)

Fig. 10.2. Students and museum staff at the British Museum
(Image: Scott Creighton)

at the time, but it was to be a trip filled with a quite unexpected and highly significant discovery.

After a couple of false starts searching the museum for Usick's department, we eventually met with her at the museum's information desk, and she led us to the Egyptian and Near East Department's study room (fig. 10.2) via an incredibly tortuous labyrinth through the museum. Indeed, from the information desk it took us a full ten minutes to finally arrive at the study room, having passed through a number of long passageways, expansive hallways, and galleries, through a number of doors, up some stairs, through some other small rooms, down in a service elevator, and finally into the room where Hill's facsimile drawings were at last presented to us.

All around us there were numerous students and museum staff members employed in analyzing and cataloguing all manner of ancient artifacts. Usick led us to the room where Hill's facsimile drawings, filed in a protective binder, had been laid out on a long table. Photography of the material was permitted so long as we did not use a flash.

The elaborately decorated protective folder (fig. 10.3) was about

Exhibit 6 • The Lie of the Landscapes 117

Fig. 10.3. The reverse side of the protective folder containing the Hill facsimiles in the British Museum (Image: Scott Creighton)

two feet wide by three feet long. A cream-colored panel on the front of the folder detailed the contents therein; it was written in an elaborate, cursive handwriting style and was signed at the bottom "Colonel Howard Vyse" and below this, "1837."

When finally we were able to view all twenty-eight of Hill's facsimile drawings, they told their own story and confirmed my suspicions about Vyse's horizontally aligned diary entries of the Khufu cartouche—that the Khufu cartouche drawn by Vyse in his private journal had been copied from an original secret source that had been oriented *horizontally* when Vyse and Hill first found and copied it.

But how was it possible to reach this conclusion from only a brief study of Hill's drawings? The realization began to dawn when Louise picked up one of the facsimiles and was confused as to which way it should be held up in order for me to photograph the facsimile sheet with the correct orientation of the hieroglyphs as they would have appeared to someone standing in the chamber observing and copying them. The hieroglyphs on this particular facsimile drawing were oriented 90° to the signatures of the various witnesses, including Hill's signature (fig. 10.4, p. 118.)

J. R. Hill

Fig. 10.4. Artist's impression of Hill facsimile showing hieroglyphs oriented 90° to Hill's signature (and other signatures on original). This is how the hieroglyphs appear to an observer standing or crouching in the chamber. The facsimile sheet (and the hieroglyphs thereon) is given the correct orientation by the signature of Hill (and the other signatories). When Hill's signature is the correct way up then the hieroglyphs on the sheet will take on their chamber orientation. (Image: Scott Creighton, based on original drawing by J. R. Hill)

I explained to Louise that many of the hieroglyphs in these chambers of the Great Pyramid were, in fact, painted onto the stone blocks upside-down or sideways. I further explained that Hill's signature, as well as the signatures of the other witnesses found on the facsimile sheets, effectively served as a compass, telling us the proper orientation of the facsimile sheet and thus of the hieroglyphs as they would be observed in the chamber; that is, the witness signatures and attestations should always be the right way up (like the north indicator on a map), thereby rotating the hieroglyphs on the sheet to their actual orientation within the chamber.

So we carried on, carefully photographing each of Hill's facsimile drawings, ensuring that the signatures and attestations on the facsimile sheets were the right way up so that we could photograph the hiero-

Exhibit 6 • The Lie of the Landscapes 119

glyphs with the correct chamber orientation. When we had finished our work and were checking the drawings on our laptops against the plan drawings made by Perring,[1] the penny dropped, and I finally realized what had been nagging my mind for the best part of a year.

In Hill's facsimile drawing of the Khufu cartouche that I had seen the year before, it had been signed with the wrong chamber orientation (relative to Hill's signature). This was the same for the other part of this gang name that was drawn by Hill on a separate facsimile sheet. This is to say that, almost without exception, when reading Hill's signature upright on the various facsimile drawings from the relieving chambers, we find that twenty-two of the twenty-four facsimile drawings that we were able to cross-check are correctly oriented with respect to the orientation of the actual quarry marks within the chambers. From a binomial statistical probability perspective, for Hill's signature to correctly lock in the orientation of twenty-two from twenty-four* facsimiles purely by random chance is practically zero. This strongly suggests that Hill had a clear system of using his own signature (and those of other witnesses) as a "this way up" sign to lock in the correct relative orientation of each set of quarry marks that he painted onto each facsimile sheet.

The two incorrect facsimile orientations consisted of the gang name "Companions of Khufu" from Campbell's Chamber and are presented over two sheets, both of which were signed by Hill (the *only* witness) as though he had been copying these particular quarry marks from an original source that had the glyphs oriented *horizontally* (fig. 10.5, p. 120), thereby providing corroboration that this gang name facsimile painted by Hill had come from some other place outside the Great Pyramid where the source had a different orientation (i.e., horizontal) to what we actually find in Campbell's Chamber (i.e., rotated 90°). It seems then that Hill copied these marks from that source and unwittingly and

---

*It should be noted that we could cross-check the orientations of twenty-four of the twenty-eight facsimiles against Perring's plan drawing because Hill had drawn some signs that Perring had missed [and vice versa], and thus the orientations on those four other drawings could not be compared. Also, the orientations of some of Hill's drawings were compared against some fairly recent photos of the glyphs made by Colette Dowell and Robert Schoch, for which we were grateful.

J. R. Hill

*Fig. 10.5. Artist impression of Hill facsimile of Khufu
cartouche with (mock) Hill signature in "landscape"
(Image: Scott Creighton)*

habitually signed the bottom of the landscape facsimile sheet (as most
artists do), aligning his signature with, and locking in, the *horizontal*
orientation of the original source, just as he used his signature to do so
for all the other drawings that he made.

This is to say that, had Hill made this facsimile drawing from the
vertically aligned Khufu cartouche that we observe today in Campbell's
Chamber, then, by following the signing convention he clearly employed
with every other facsimile drawing (that we were able to check) to lock
in the chamber orientation of these marks with his signature then he
should have signed his Khufu facsimile sheet in a position to indicate
that he had observed these drawings vertically in Campbell's Chamber,
as shown in figure 10.6.

That Hill appears not to have followed his own signing convention
with regard to these particular facsimiles strongly suggests that these
drawings had originally been copied from some alternative source where
Hill *did,* in fact, follow his normal signing convention; he instinctively
and habitually signed the drawing as he normally would, at the foot
of the horizontal/landscape drawing (fig. 10.5), because that *was* the
orientation of the *original* source cartouche. That Hill then, rather
stupidly, decided to rotate his already signed landscape drawing 90°
to copy it into the Great Pyramid was to be his undoing, as this decision resulted in the very obvious discrepancy that we find today with
his signature. Had Hill simply copied this drawing into the chamber

Exhibit 6 • The Lie of the Landscapes   121

Fig. 10.6. Artist impression of vertically/sideways aligned Khufu cartouche with (mock) Hill signature at bottom right of sheet (Image: Scott Creighton)

horizontally, then his deception would have gone entirely unnoticed.

It seems somewhat ironic that Hill's signature was placed on his facsimile drawings in order to vouch for the authenticity of the hieroglyphs in these chambers, yet it is his signature that has, in the end, been his undoing as once again the truth of these marks in Campbell's Chamber of the Great Pyramid is laid bare. And it has to be said—if Vyse and his team could fake even a *single* mark in these chambers, then their action taints *all* the marks found in Campbell's Chamber and all the chambers below; this evidence becomes the fruit of the poisonous tree.

CHAPTER TEN SUMMARY

• In Vyse's private journal we find that he draws the Suphis/Khufu cartouche no less than *three* times in a horizontal fashion. This is odd for two reasons: first, the actual cartouche in Campbell's Chamber is aligned vertically, and second, Vyse draws all other cartouches in his diary with their actual orientation; that is, as they would appear to someone standing in the various chambers observing the cartouches. Why then, when he maintains the chamber

orientation of other drawings, would Vyse draw the Khufu cartouche in his private journal with a different orientation from how
it actually appears in Campbell's Chamber?

- Hill was tasked by Vyse to make facsimile drawings of all the markings found inside the various chambers. Hill made a total of twenty-
eight facsimile drawings.

- From an analysis of his drawings, Hill clearly deployed a system of
using his signature as a "this way up" sign to lock in the chamber
orientation of each facsimile sheet. With his signature (and those of
some of the other witnesses) always upright, this would effectively
record and lock in the chamber orientation of a particular drawing,
allowing us to know exactly how the signs appeared when someone
was standing and observing them in a particular chamber; that is,
they would then appear on the facsimile sheet upright, sideways, or
even upside-down.

- Of Hill's twenty-eight facsimiles, the orientations of twenty-four
were cross-checked with other sources.

- Two drawings did not conform to this convention employed
by Hill—drawings of the "Friends of Khufu" gang name from
Campbell's Chamber. This may be the smoking gun—that Hill
actually copied this gang name with its associated Khufu cartouche
from another source where it *had* been orientated horizontally,
which is why Hill automatically and instinctively signed the two
drawings with that particular orientation.

- When Hill then copied this facsimile image into Campbell's
Chamber, it was rotated 90° (to fit onto a single, inclined roof
block), thereby creating this inconsistency with his signature.

- Hill's signature, used to testify that each drawing was a true facsimile copy of the original, unwittingly serves to indicate a fraud.

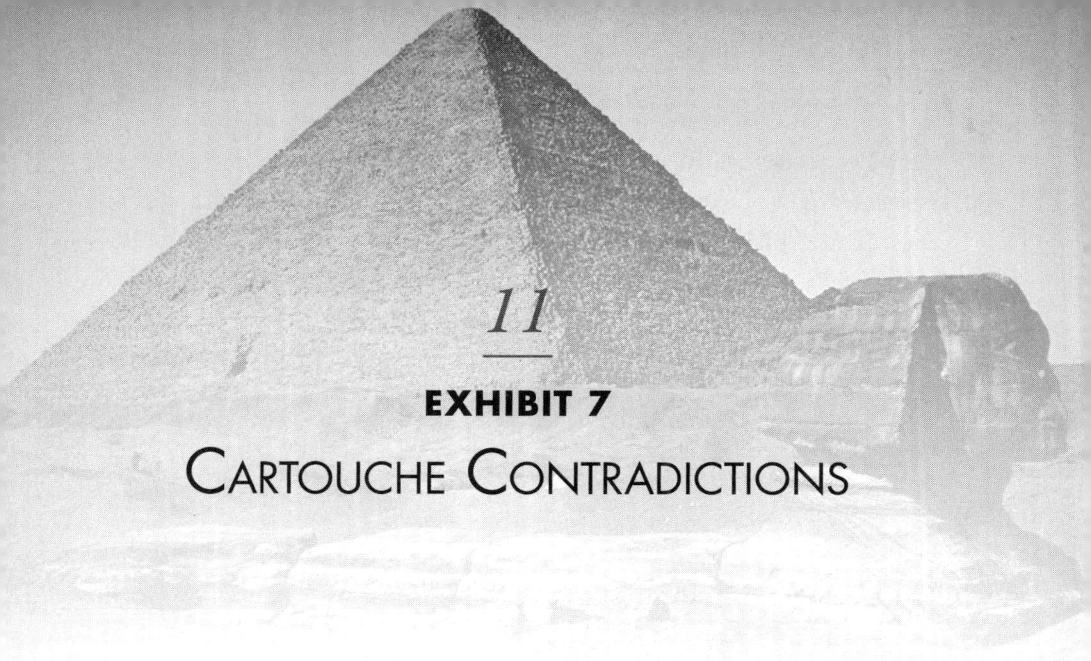

EXHIBIT 7

CARTOUCHE CONTRADICTIONS

Throughout the course of this book we have learned that it is the view of Egyptologists that the painted marks within the hidden chambers of the Great Pyramid were Fourth Dynasty graffiti—crude hieroglyphs painted onto stone blocks by the various work gangs working the stone at the quarries. Egyptologists do not believe that the quarry marks on the blocks within these chambers were made in situ; that is, once the wall and roof blocks had been set in place. However, the evidence thus far presented suggests this to be an erroneous view. In this chapter additional evidence will be presented that further supports the hypothesis that these painted markings were created in situ by nineteenth-century hoaxers.

No fraud is ever perfect, and even the best fraudster will make mistakes, leaving behind subtle clues to their deception—it's an occupational hazard. Often these mistakes will go undetected for many decades and even centuries. In 1837, Vyse and his small team lived in a world without electrical lighting or cameras. There were no robotics or endoscopic devices to scan inaccessible places within the chambers. And there was no internet. In this pre-Victorian world, Vyse could never, in his wildest dreams, have imagined the intense scrutiny that modern technology would bring to bear on the painted marks he claimed to have discovered in these chambers. All of these technological marvels of the modern world have allowed the painted marks on the walls of these chambers to enter the homes of millions all over the world. These chambers are no longer the remote and

relatively inaccessible places that they were in 1837; their content no longer
the preserve of the academic establishment who accept, almost without
question, the authenticity of these markings on what, in the end, amounts
to nothing more than the word and the "good character" of Vyse. But in
their haste to perpetrate a convincing fraud, Vyse and his team *did* make
a number of mistakes; a number of subtle clues left behind in these chambers and, in particular, the top-most Campbell's Chamber that point to
their deception. Let us now consider this further evidence.

BLOCK ORIENTATION

As noted previously, the conventional view of the 90° rotated alignment
of the gang name glyphs (which encompasses the Khufu cartouche) on
the inclined roof block of Campbell's Chamber (fig. 1.9, p. 9) is that
these marks were painted onto a regular rectangular block while the
block was lying horizontally at the quarry. When the block eventually
arrived at the pyramid, it was then rotated and set upright (at around
30° from the horizontal plane) into the gabled roof, thus the horizontally painted quarry marks were now effectively rotated 90° and now
appear vertically aligned on the chamber roof trussing (fig. 11.1). This

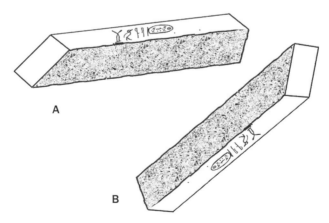

*Fig. 11.1. (A) Gang name is painted onto a quarried block while it is
lying horizontal at the quarry; (B) the painted block is then rotated 90°,
inclined to around 30°, and set into the roof of Campbell's Chamber.
(Image: Scott Creighton)*

Exhibit 7 • Cartouche Contradictions 125

all seems very reasonable and perfectly plausible—until we take a much closer examination of these roof blocks.

There is an inherent problem with this particular conventional scenario that attempts to explain the orientation of the quarry marks on this roof block of Campbell's Chamber, and it relates to the *shape* of the roof blocks. Unlike most rectangular-shaped core blocks of the Great Pyramid, the roof blocks of Campbell's Chamber have an inherent, in-built orientation that is entirely separate from its positioning within the chamber. Artifacts such as an obelisk, a fluted pillar, a stele, a storage pot, a vertical writing register or even an anthropoid coffin lid all possess an inherent "top end" or "upness." In this regard the roof blocks of Campbell's Chamber are no different. This is because one end of each of these roof blocks is uniquely shaped, *tapered* to facilitate an adjoining roof block, thus creating a triangular support trussing (see fig. 9.1, p. 106). The tapered or gabled end of these roof blocks, like the pointed end of an obelisk, is akin to having a *this-way-up* sign built into these blocks right at the quarry. Regular, rectangular blocks have no inherent this-way-up sign and, as such, have no in-built orientation—either end of a regular-shaped block can be regarded as the top (or bottom) end (fig. 11.2).

It must surely stand to reason, then, that the quarry gangs crafting these roof blocks would most certainly have been aware which end of such a block was the top (the tapered end) and which was the bottom

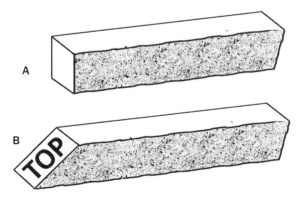

Fig. 11.2. (A) Regular rectangular quarried blocks have no inherent "top" orientation; (B) the tapered roof blocks of Campbell's Chamber have an "in-built" orientation, a "top" end. (Image: Scott Creighton)

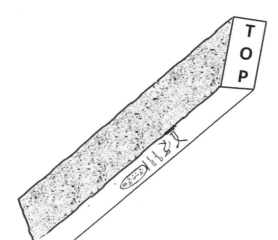

Fig. 11.3. The quarry marks are painted onto the roof block in Campbell's Chamber perpendicular to the top end of the roof block. (Image: Scott Creighton)

(the non-tapered end). As such, it makes little sense to find that, with this understanding, an ancient Egyptian scribe would go against normal ancient Egyptian writing convention (a convention that we find on all other top-ended artifacts) and paint these gang name signs perpendicular to the block's inherent top orientation; that is, rotated 90° to the block's in-built "upness" (fig. 11.3).

On no other ancient Egyptian artifact with a clearly defined top end do we find inscriptions rotated in such a way as we find on these long, gabled roof blocks in Campbell's Chamber. On any fluted column, obelisk, stele, storage pot, anthropoid coffin lid (i.e., artifacts with a clearly defined top end), we find that written signs, whether they be monumental or mundane, simple or complex, are written *always* with the top of each sign aligning with the top end of the particular artifact (fig. 11.4).

Given that the scribe would surely have known where the top of each gabled roof block was, then, in keeping with their grammatical rules, it surely would have been more natural for the scribe to write his signs onto such long blocks in *columns* with the top of each sign aligned with the top end of the roof block as in figure 11.5. This is all the more so

Exhibit 7 • Cartouche Contradictions 127

Fig. 11.4. Artifacts with a clearly defined "top" have the top of each sign aligned to the top of the artifact. (Image: Scott Creighton)

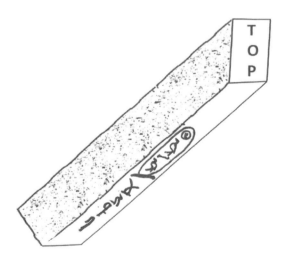

Fig. 11.5. Example of how the quarry marks should have been placed onto the roof block of Campbell's Chamber to conform to the grammatical rules of ancient Egyptian writing on a stone artifact with a clearly defined top. (Image: Scott Creighton)

given that, up until the end of the Eleventh Dynasty, strings of hieratic texts such as these would normally be written in *columns* and *not* in the horizontal rows we find on all the blocks in these chambers.[1] That not a single string of hieratic text is presented in column format within any of the chambers opened by Vyse is surely peculiar and even more so given that the column format of gang names from this period has been found elsewhere outside the Great Pyramid (see fig. 12.5). By further comparison, if we compare the signs in the old hieratic papyri ("Merer's diary") found in 2013 at Wadi al-Jarf we immediately find that the hieratic text is laid out in column format (as would be expected for this period) and that the chisel and quail chick hieratic signs (used in Khufu's gang name in Campbell's Chamber) in this papyri find their best match with Goedicke's paleography around the Fourth Dynasty period.

In short then, with this "top-end" knowledge of these roof blocks it is, therefore, unlikely in the extreme that an ancient Egyptian scribe would place the gang name (including the king's cartouche) onto the block in the perpendicular/horizontal manner that we see within the Great Pyramid today but would, instead, have painted the markings onto the block *upright* in a column that was more common for this period as shown in the examples in figures 11.5 and 12.5.

But this is precisely the sort of subtle detail that even the best forger might easily overlook, because the top end (the wedge) of these roof blocks are not actually visible within the chamber and, therefore, such a thought would unlikely have crossed the minds of the forgers—they treated the roof blocks as though they were regular, rectangular blocks (like the chamber wall blocks) and, in so doing, left behind a massive clue to their deception.

PAINT OVERLAP

Further evidence of in-situ painting of the Khufu cartouche arises from the observations of independent researcher and art expert Jon Snape, MA. As noted, it is believed that this gang name (including the Khufu cartouche) was painted onto this roof block when it was lying horizontally at the quarry. Given that hieratic marks in this early Old Kingdom

Exhibit 7 • Cartouche Contradictions   129

period were usually written (and read) from right to left (and usually in columns), this means that the cartouche in this gang name would have been painted onto the block *first* (right to left when the block is lying horizontal at the quarry) and the *apr* sign (fig. 11.1A) painted *last*. The evidence, however, points to these marks having been painted onto this roof block by someone more used to our Western writing convention; that is, from left to right (thereby top-to-bottom painting of an in-situ block).

Snape points out that a close examination of the paint tracks between the top of the Khufu cartouche oval and the horizontal reed stroke (fig. 11.6, *top*) shows that the arc of the cartouche oval has been painted slightly *into and over* the horizontal reed stroke at the top of the oval.[2] This means that the higher positioned reed stroke must have been painted *before* the lower positioned cartouche oval that, if these are genuine hieratic marks painted from right to left on a block lying horizontally at the quarry, makes no sense whatsoever as the top of the oval should surely then be *under* the reed stroke. This observation by Snape makes sense *only* if these marks were painted onto the roof block from left to right (i.e., top to bottom of the in-situ, vertical roof block),

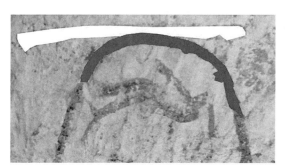

Fig. 11.6. The paint tracks of the arc of the cartouche oval (top) overlaps the paint of the horizontal reed stroke implying top-down in-situ painting of these signs. Overlap highlighted (bottom). (Photo: Patrick Chapuis. Highlight: Scott Creighton)

in which case the reed stroke is painted from the *left* and *before* the cartouche oval and thus presents us with further evidence of fakery.

THE PAINT RUNNELS

In 2005 the French photographer Patrick Chapuis presented one of the most stunning high-resolution photographs ever taken of the Khufu cartouche in Campbell's Chamber. This remarkable photograph revealed some quite astonishing features of the painted cartouche, features that had, hitherto, gone completely unnoticed.

Using the Chapuis photograph along with some others published online by Colette Dowell, Ph.D., Snape further showed that the Khufu cartouche was painted by starting at the bottom-right corner of the cartouche oval.[3] It is in this area of the cartouche that we find the red ochre paint is most concentrated (fig. 11.7). The cartouche, from this bottom-right point, was drawn upward and around counterclockwise, and the paint gradually becomes thinner as the brush moves around the cartouche to its finishing point at the bottom left.

A close examination of the Khufu cartouche on the roof block of Campbell's Chamber reveals something quite peculiar. At the bottom-right section of this cartouche where the paint is most concentrated,

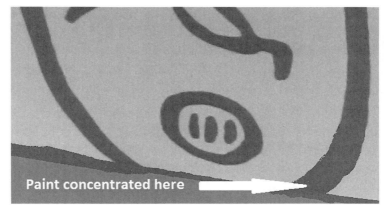

Fig. 11.7. Artist's impression of Khufu cartouche showing that the red paint is most concentrated at the bottom right of the cartouche. (Image: Scott Creighton)

Exhibit 7 • Cartouche Contradictions   131

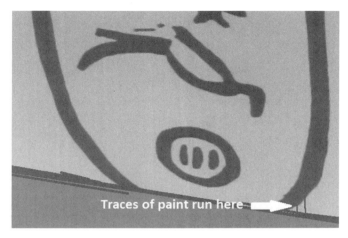

*Fig. 11.8. Artist's impression of the Khufu cartouche on the
vertical roof trussing of Campbell's Chamber shows traces of
red paint running vertically down the block from the bottom
right of the cartouche where the paint is most concentrated.
(Image: Scott Creighton)*

traces of two paint runnels can be observed running vertically down the
roof block (fig. 11.8).

Furthermore, where the cartouche roof block meets the low support
wall, traces of red paint (presumably from the vertical paint runnels) can
be observed spreading out laterally along the joint (fig. 11.9, p. 132). Also,
just to the bottom left of the cartouche, as pointed out by independent
researcher Philip Femano, Ph.D., the roof block appears to have been
scraped in a long horizontal line (not shown here) as though to remove
something from the surface of the roof block. Could this be evidence of
a botched paint job where unwanted paint had trickled down from the
bottom-right section of the cartouche, where the paint was at its thickest, and spread out along the joint of the low support wall?

What these paint runnels seem to indicate, of course, is that this
gang name with its cartouche, contrary to what Egyptologists state,
was actually painted *in situ;* that is, *not* when the block was cut at the
quarry, but *after* the block was set in place. One might not immediately
understand the implication of such an observation, but the simple fact

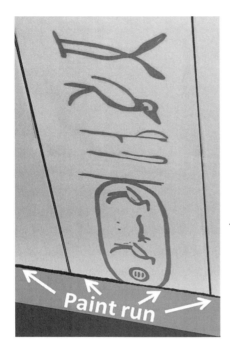

Fig. 11.9. Reproduction of Khufu cartouche on chamber roof block. Traces of red paint have spread laterally along the roof-wall joint. (Image: Scott Creighton)

Fig. 11.10. A vertically aligned Khufu cartouche painted in situ would have the signs presented upright and not rotated sideways. (Image: Scott Creighton)

Exhibit 7 • Cartouche Contradictions 133

is that this finding, all by itself, proves beyond reasonable doubt that this cartouche must then be a modern fake.

We know this because the ancient Egyptian scribes would *never* have painted this gang name in situ in the manner that we observe it, with the signs rotated 90° (i.e., sideways). Were an ancient Egyptian scribe to have painted this gang name in situ, then the reed bar of the cartouche would have been placed at the bottom of the cartouche oval (not the top), and the characters within the vertical cartouche would have been painted standing upright (as in fig. 11.10).

In short, whoever painted the gang name (including the Khufu cartouche) that we observe today in Campbell's Chamber painted it onto the roof block in such a way as to give the *impression* that it had not been painted in situ, but the telltale runnels of paint entirely contradict this notion. And if this gang name was painted in situ (as the paint evidence strongly suggests), then it has clearly been faked, because, as stated, an ancient Egyptian scribe would *never* have painted an in-situ gang name in this manner.

PAINT SPOTS

Just about every drawing of the Khufu cartouche from Campbell's Chamber presents two small dots aligned side by side, just under the snake, or horned viper, hieroglyph (fig. 10.5, p. 120). Indeed, even in the first drawings of this cartouche made by Vyse (in his private journal), Hill, and Perring, we observe these two small dots placed below the snake sign. They are repeated time and time again in the various drawings produced by these men, although Perring, in his final drawing, failed to include them, perhaps realizing by this time that these two small dots were not in fact hieroglyphic signs and thus not actually part of the king's name. However, given the relatively poor understanding of ancient Egyptian hieroglyphics and hieratic script in 1837, one might forgive these early explorers for believing that these two dots under the snake hieroglyph were part of the king's name. It would have been natural to think such a thing.

Or would it?

Fig. 11.11. Reproduction of Khufu cartouche showing random paint spots in and around the cartouche. Why, when making their copies of this cartouche, did Vyse and Hill feel compelled to reproduce only the two side-by-side spots of paint under the snake sign? (Image: Scott Creighton)

When we have a close look at the cartouche photographs made by Chapuis, Dowell, and Schoch, we can easily see that there are countless other small spots of paint all over the Khufu gang name, particularly the cartouche. Some of these paint spots are smaller than the two paint spots under the snake sign, while many are larger (fig. 11.11).

The question is, Why, when seeing all of these other small spots of paint scattered all over this cartouche, did Vyse and Hill identify only these two particular paint spots under the snake sign as being of significance? Why not any of the other paint spots? Indeed, why copy *any* of these paint spots as it would surely have been obvious to Vyse and Hill that the two paint spots below the snake sign were no more significant than any of the other countless paint spots in and around this cartouche and, as such, deserved no special attention?

For some bizarre reason, Vyse and Hill—on a number of occasions—saw reason to pick out and draw these two unremarkable paint spots in their own drawings. Why would they have considered that these two particular dots under the snake glyph had sufficient significance that would so compel them both to include them in their drawings of this cartouche?

Exhibit 7 • Cartouche Contradictions 135

There is one possibility that might explain such a peculiar action. This book contends that Vyse discovered a master cache of inscriptions that contained, inter alia, Khufu's various names and that Vyse subsequently copied the inscriptions into the various chambers he opened within the Great Pyramid. If we were to suppose that Vyse's master Khufu cartouche had two small dots under the snake sign (perhaps accidental drops of paint or ink) and that these were the *only* spots on his master drawing, then it is quite likely (and understandable) that Vyse would in such a circumstance have believed that the two dots (the *only* dots) were a fully intended part of the king's name and, as such, would have copied them in good faith, not realizing at this time that he was actually copying superfluous marks. These superfluous marks were then replicated in Campbell's Chamber, in Vyse's private journal (several times), and in Hill's facsimile drawing.

It seems, though, that Vyse later realized that the two dots were not, in fact, part of the king's name, for in his published book he presents the drawing made by Perring in which he had now omitted these two dots from the Khufu cartouche, perhaps logically reasoning (as Vyse and Hill surely also should have done) that these two dots were just random splashes of paint that had no more significance than any of the other paint splashes.

THE PEBBLES

Further analysis of the Suphis/Khufu cartouche in Campbell's Chamber presents even more striking evidence that this cartouche appears to have been faked.

Close examination of the cartouche reveals numerous small pebbles stuck onto the surface of the roof block. These small pebbles can be seen scattered right across the gang name (most especially the cartouche), sometimes in small clusters, sometimes individually, as shown in the images in figure 11.12 on p. 136.

Within the painted areas of the cartouche it can be observed that the pebbles have been painted over with the red ochre paint, which allows us to deduce that these pebbles were somehow affixed to the

a

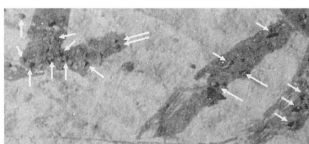

b

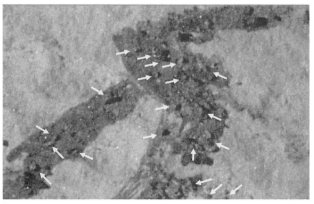

c

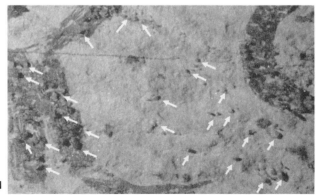

d

Fig. 11.12. Photos of the Khufu cartouche showing clusters of small pebbles affixed to the surface of the roof block (arrows). Red paint can be observed on top of some of the pebbles. (Image: Patrick Chapuis)

Exhibit 7 • Cartouche Contradictions 137

roof block *before* the block was painted. Even in the *unpainted* areas of this roof block (fig. 11.12d) we find that small clusters of pebbles are affixed to the roof block but, obviously, have not been coated with the red ochre paint.

One might reasonably ask why any of this matters. The answer to that question lies in how these clusters of pebbles managed to affix themselves to a sloping, inclined block of Tura limestone. These small pebbles can't just attach themselves to such an inclined block by themselves; they need a bonding agent, a strong adhesive of some kind. The most likely adhesive that would be strong enough is lime slurry—a thin plaster mix. The roof blocks of Campbell's Chamber weigh around sixty tons—or thereabouts—and moving such heavy weights is not at all easy. The ancient builders would have needed all the help they could get. To assist in the moving of such a heavy block the ancient builders would often use lime slurry as a lubricant to reduce the friction of the block as it was being maneuvered into its final position (as noted in chapter 9). Traces of this slurry were found on the stone blocks throughout the relief chambers as well as in the Descending Passage of the Great Pyramid, where it is believed to have been introduced to help facilitate the slipping of three granite plugs down the passageway to block access to the upper chambers of the pyramid. We find it also within the grooves of the "granite leaf" block within the Ante Chamber of the Great Pyramid.

As the block was being moved through the slurry, pieces of grit and small pebbles would be trapped and become affixed to the surface of the block as it is slid into place and would effectively become cemented onto the raised surface of the block as the slurry lubricant dried and hardened, acting like a thin plaster.

All of which, of course, begs the obvious question: If the block was dragged through a lime slurry mix and small stones became affixed to the surface of the block, how is it that we can see the gang name (and its cartouche) so clearly? Surely, if these marks had been painted onto the block before it was set in place, then these quarry marks would have been totally obliterated by being dragged through the lime slurry lubricant. At the very least, we would only be able to perhaps observe faint traces of the quarry marks, as they would have been almost completely smeared and coated with the lime slurry, the same lubricant that caused the small pebbles to become affixed to the surface of the block.

It is noticeable, though, that these small pebbles appear to be concentrated in the painted areas (i.e., concentrated within the brush strokes of the painted signs), and, as such, it has been argued that the red ochre paint itself may have acted as the bonding agent. However, experimental research conducted by myself shows this to be highly unlikely. Water-based red ochre paint simply does not possess sufficient bonding strength to hold such small pebbles in place, breaking loose with just the slightest of touches. By contrast, further experimental research has shown that plaster slurry can solidly hold such small pebbles to the block's surface. The higher concentration of pebbles observed in the painted areas of these marks may simply be the result of maintenance of the chamber by the Egyptian authorities that is known to have taken place, brushing away detritus from the unpainted areas of the block while, naturally, avoiding touching the precious painted areas. Over time the effect of this produces a higher concentration of these small pebbles in the painted areas of the block's surface.

The fact remains—the Chapuis photograph of these painted marks shows small stones affixed to the inclined roof block in painted areas *and* unpainted areas, a situation that is easily explained in *both* instances by invoking the use of a strong bonding agent such as a thin lime slurry, which we know the ancient Egyptians used to help slide such heavy blocks into place.

What this tells us, once again, is that these particular quarry marks—the gang name and its cartouche—were obviously painted onto this roof trussing only *after* the block had been set in place. And, that being the case, then it is simply inconceivable that an ancient Egyptian scribe would have painted the gang name onto this in-situ roof block with the signs rotated sideways; these glyphs, painted onto an in-situ block, would most certainly have been painted into the vertical cartouche in an *upright* fashion as in figure 11.10.

Exhibit 7 • Cartouche Contradictions 139

THE PLASTER

Conventional thought with regards to the gabled roof blocks of Campbell's Chamber informs us that they are made of a fine white limestone hewn from the quarries at Tura. The facts above notwithstanding, any white plaster slurry applied to the surface of a white limestone block would make it, through simple observation alone, somewhat difficult to tell if there was a white plaster layer applied to the surface of the white limestone block. In consideration of this dilemma, in November 2015, I contacted Dominique Görlitz (via video link), who, in 2013 (along with Stefan Erdmann), had removed a small sample of ochre paint (fig. 11.13) from one of the glyphs in Campbell's Chamber (*not* from the Khufu cartouche) intending to have the sample chemically analyzed by a German laboratory to determine its mineral composition.

Görlitz and Erdmann had hoped to have the paint sample radiocarbon dated to determine its age (from the organic material sometimes added to ancient ochre paint as a binding agent) and thus to determine

Fig. 11.13. Photo of a quarry mark on a roof block in Campbell's Chamber showing area (circled) where ochre paint (and block surface) was removed by Görlitz and Erdmann for scientific analysis. (Photo: Dominique Görlitz)

the pyramid's age. Alas, however, the ochre paint sample size was insufficient for radiocarbon testing to proceed. However, the laboratory was able to provide Görlitz and Erdmann with other information regarding the mineral composition of the material the ochre paint had been painted onto; that is, the immediate subsurface behind the ochre paint. If this ochre paint had indeed been painted directly onto a limestone surface, as conventional opinion insists, then the chemical analysis of the block material immediately *behind* the ochre paint sample should have shown its mineral composition to consist of calcium carbonate—limestone. But it did not. In our video discussion (later confirmed to me by e-mail), Görlitz explained that the laboratory analysis found that the mineral composition of the surface material his ochre paint sample had been painted onto was *not* calcium carbonate (limestone) but rather calcium sulfate—*plaster.* No evidence of calcium carbonate was reported from the test sample analysis. This finding supports the proposition that a thin, plaster slurry was used to slide the blocks into their final position and that this same plaster slurry could have resulted in some small pebbles bonding to the block's surface, as shown in figure 11.12a–d.

It should be noted here, in the interests of clarity, that it is known that some plaster repair works appear to have been carried out in this area of the chamber. However, the ochre paint sample removed by Görlitz and Erdmann had no plaster on *top* of the ochre paint they removed—the plaster the laboratory analysis found was from the material directly *behind* the paint sample. It is also known that limestone blocks can exude tiny trace elements of calcium sulfate. Typically, this will, on average, amount to around 0.038 percent[4] of a given sample. Such a tiny trace element would have virtually zero bearing on the limestone's hardness, with limestone having a mohs rating of 3.5 and calcium sulfate, a much softer substance, a mohs rating of 2. In their tests, Görlitz explained to me that the sample they removed was found to be much softer than natural limestone and entirely consistent with plaster. There is little doubt, then, that these hieratic signs were painted onto a surface of thin plaster.

But the laboratory's scientific analysis did not end there. An analysis of a number of rectangular-shaped patina markings found on the granite underside of the King's Chamber ceiling within the Great Pyramid

Exhibit 7 • Cartouche Contradictions   141

revealed that the mineral composition of these dark patches consisted of an oxide of iron known as "magnetite." While most metamorphic and igneous rocks such as granite contain small traces of this mineral, the concentration of magnetite found through scientific analysis of these patina strips was far in excess of naturally occurring concentrations, and their regular shape on the roof blocks of the King's Chamber would seem to lend strong support to the view that the builders of this structure had access to iron tools.

As Görlitz explained to me in a private e-mail:

We investigated the Aswan granite from the King's Chamber which definitely does not contain magnetite in a measurable concentration. Even more important is the way this magnetite patina was discovered. Each beam on the King's Chamber ceiling contains this patina in the same size, color and appearance. Always against each other and at the same position.

This arrangement led me to the conclusion (before we made our metallurgical investigation) that this pattern must have been caused by an anthropogenic activity/effect. Furthermore, when I first saw this patina, I could see a black metallic glimmer which could never be the result of geometabolism but was clearly the result of an interaction between a "metal" and the granite stone!

Later in the laboratory we could detect by micro analysis and XPS, a huge concentration of Fe_3O_4 (magnetite) and further iron oxides which clearly points to a layer which was formed by a stone-iron interaction. In cooperation with iron experts of the Technical University of Freiberg/Saxony, their analysis of the material confirmed my hypothesis that an "unknown" iron tool must have been used during the erecting of this chamber! (Incidentally, pure granite contains Fe_2O—hematite but no magnetite.)

This discovery changes our perception of the materials used in antiquity and thus we have to reevaluate our concepts about the technical development of the 4th Dynasty . . . the ancient Egyptians might have lifted their giant blocks without the use of ramps. The iron discovery allows the use of simple blades which worked as a protection for the brittle granite beams. Furthermore, the workers could use wedges in order to push up the beams from layer to layer, just as Herodotus described. . . .

In a large lifting experiment I was able to prove this hypothesis experimentally. Only two people were needed to raise a 16 ton block. It is not proof as such but it delivers an empirical argument that the written ancient records from Herodotus might be true. . . .

Returning to the issue of the plaster—given that it is inconceivable in the extreme that ancient Egyptian quarry workers would apply a layer of plaster to any block at the quarry, paint, and then transport it, we have to accept that the plaster was applied to the gabled roof blocks when in situ; that is, after or just as the block was being maneuvered into its final inclined position in the pyramid, perhaps by sliding it through a thin plaster slurry to reduce friction. And thus, as previously stated, we then have to ask why any ancient Egyptian scribe, with an inclined roof block (essentially a sloping wall) in front of them, would decide to paint markings onto such a "wall" in a *sideways* manner. Surely, when writing a piece of text onto such an inclined surface we would still write our text upright.

This rotation of the quarry marks is, of course, the kind of "trick" a determined forger would employ to make the marks *seem* genuine; a rotational trick that forces us to conclude that the marks *must* have been painted at the quarry, ergo, *must* be authentic. The empirical scientific evidence, however, strongly suggests otherwise.

THE PENCIL

Once again, the high-resolution photography of Patrick Chapuis revealed another extraordinary feature of the Khufu cartouche within Campbell's Chamber, a feature that is barely perceptible on most other photographs of the cartouche. This was first brought to my attention by independent researcher Audrey Mulertt in early September 2014, after she noticed that the Khufu cartouche in Campbell's Chamber had been overlaid with a pencil grid, much like an artist's drawing grid (fig. 11.14).

Exhibit 7 • Cartouche Contradictions　143

This pencil grid is a complete mystery. No one, either in mainstream or alternative circles, seems to know how, why, or when this grid appeared in the Khufu cartouche, although even in some of the earliest photographs of the cartouche, made by the Egyptologist Rainer Stadelmann in the 1990s, the pencil grid can be seen, though only just.

But what could the purpose of such a grid have been? In the art world such grids are sometimes used when an artist has a small-scale drawing that he or she wishes to make an enlarged copy of. In this instance we can imagine that this pencil grid was drawn on the roof block of Campbell's Chamber and a similar, smaller grid was drawn on a source master. The grid drawn over the smaller source drawing acts as a guide to enlarge the drawing, using the enlarged grid, on the roof block. The question we have to ask now is whether this pencil grid went *over* the painted hieroglyphs or *under* them.

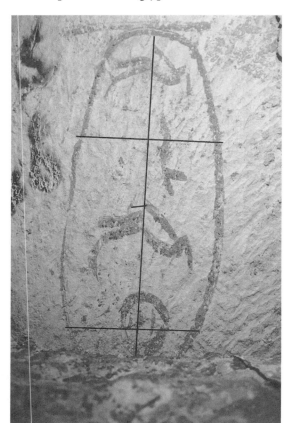

Fig. 11.14. Photo of the Khufu cartouche showing the (enhanced) pencil "drawing grid" (Photo: Patrick Chapuis. Grid enhancement: Scott Creighton)

Because the ancient Egyptians did not have graphite pencils, it stands to reason that if these pencil lines are *under* the red ochre paint, the painted hieroglyphs must be relatively modern and thus fake. If, however, the pencil lines are found to be on *top* of the paint, all that would establish is that the pencil grid lines were drawn *after* the hieroglyphs had been painted onto the stone block; this may have been in ancient times or it may, as other evidence presented elsewhere in this book suggests, have been relatively recent. It is known, for example, that a number of other people, such as Perring and Egyptologist Alan Rowe, also made reduced-scale drawings of this cartouche, as did Hill with his facsimile drawings, so it is entirely possible that any of these men could have placed this pencil grid over the cartouche sometime after May 1837, when Vyse first opened this particular chamber. In her experimental research, Mulertt demonstrated that a pencil line drawn onto stone, even when painted over with various paints, can actually appear as though it has been drawn on top of the paint, as the graphite seems to bleed through the paint.[5]

It seems, then, that only modern forensic testing might be able to definitively determine whether this pencil grid line in Campbell's Chamber goes under or over the painted quarry marks of the Khufu cartouche. As stated, if the pencil lines go under the ochre paint, then the quarry marks are, unquestionably, fake. If, on the other hand, it is found that the pencil lines have been drawn over the quarry marks, then the question as to the authenticity of the painted quarry marks remains open, as the pencil lines could have been placed over the quarry marks at any time after May 1837.

CHAPTER ELEVEN SUMMARY

- The roof blocks in Campbell's Chamber, unlike the regular rectangular-shaped wall blocks in this chamber, have an inherent "top end"—a tapered end of the block that would have been created right at the quarry. As such, any writing on such a top-sided block, in accordance with all other ancient Egyptian writing, would have the top of each sign aligned with the top end of the roof block. In

Exhibit 7 • Cartouche Contradictions 145

Campbell's Chamber, however, we find that the top of each quarry mark is rotated 90° from the top end of the roof block and, as such, contradicts normal ancient Egyptian grammatical rules used for monumental or mundane inscriptions.

- Up until the Eleventh Dynasty hieratic writing was usually written vertically in columns rather than the horizontal arrangement we find on the blocks in these chambers.

- A close examination of the Khufu cartouche in Campbell's Chamber shows small traces of paint having run vertically from the bottom-right corner of the oval. These paint runnels then seem to have spread out in the joint between the roof block and the chamber support wall. This evidence suggests that this cartouche was painted in situ.

- If the Khufu cartouche was painted in situ (as the paint runnels appear to indicate), then the cartouche is clearly a fraud, because an ancient Egyptian scribe would *never* draw a vertical cartouche and then place the signs sideways within that cartouche; the signs would have been painted upright.

- The paint of the Khufu cartouche oval overlaps the paint of the reed stroke, indicating that the cartouche oval was painted last, ergo top-to-bottom writing (i.e., left-to-right writing on a horizontal block at the quarry). Ancient hieratic text is always written right-to-left.

- The Khufu cartouche in Campbell's Chamber is speckled with numerous paint spots. The random nature of these paint spots would have indicated to anyone observing this cartouche that these spots were not actually of any consequence and certainly not part of the king's name. It is surely peculiar, then, that Vyse and Hill felt compelled to draw two of these paint spots under the snake sign. Of course, if Vyse and Hill had found an original source cartouche where these two dots under the snake sign were the *only* two dots, then one can understand why they might have felt that they were part of the king's name. But it is simply inconceivable that they could have thought this given even a cursory examination of the many-dotted Khufu cartouche in Campbell's Chamber.

- In 2014 two German researchers, Dominique Görlitz and Stefan Erdmann, removed a small fragment of ochre paint from one of the signs (not the king's cartouche) in Campbell's Chamber to have it radiocarbon dated. Alas, however, the ochre sample size was inadequate for carbon-14 testing to proceed. However, the testing laboratory *was* able to determine that the chemical composition of the immediate subsurface of the ochre paint (the roof block surface), rather than being of calcium carbonate (limestone), was found, instead, to be composed of a layer of calcium sulfate (plaster). No evidence of calcium carbonate was reported from the test sample analysis.

• A close examination of the Khufu cartouche in Campbell's Chamber shows many small pebbles or pieces of grit affixed to the surface of the vertical ceiling blocks in both painted and unpainted areas. The only way in which these small stones could remain affixed to the block surface is by the use of a strong bonding agent of some kind, such as plaster. The ancient Egyptians would often use a lime slurry mix to reduce friction when moving such immense weights. When this lime slurry dried it would harden, thereby "cementing" these small stones onto the surface of the block. We have to ask, Why aren't the gang name and its cartouche smeared with the lime slurry that bonded these small stones to the block? Again we have evidence supporting the view that these marks were painted onto the roof trussing in situ. As such the cartouche and other marks are clearly fraudulent as an ancient Egyptian scribe would simply *never* place characters sideways into a vertical cartouche.

• A close inspection of the Khufu cartouche also shows that a pencil drawing grid has been placed over or under the cartouche. It is unknown when this grid was created. If the pencil lines are under the cartouche, then this would identify the cartouche as a fake, because the ancient Egyptians did not use such pencils. If the pencil line goes *over* the cartouche, then the pencil markings are clearly modern and could have been drawn by anyone who entered the chamber after it was opened in 1837.

12

EXHIBIT 8

SIGNS OUT OF TIME

We have seen in previous chapters how the Suphis/Khufu cartouche in Campbell's Chamber presents a number of anomalous features. But these are not the only anomalies we find when we consider this gang name (or the gang names from the other chambers). If we now consider all the signs within the Khufu gang name (fig. 12.1), we find something rather peculiar.

According to some Egyptologists—and they are by no means certain—the translation of this gang name from Campbell's Chamber is to be read as "The gang, friends of Khufu." Other Egyptologists interpret "friends" as "companions." The problem they have in properly interpreting these glyphs stems from the third sign (from the left), which resembles our letter *q;* some Egyptologist believe this to be

Fig. 12.1. Artist's impression of the Khufu gang name from Campbell's Chamber (rotated 90° counterclockwise from chamber original) (Image: Scott Creighton, based on original drawings by J. R. Hill)

147

Fig. 12.2. A chisel sign (dashed box) from Menkaure's pyramid complex (Image: Scott Creighton, based on original drawing by Alan Rowe)

the ancient Egyptian hieratic "chisel" sign, while others, such as Zahi Hawass, consider it to be a different sign entirely. The reason for the doubt is partially understandable when we consider that the chisel sign in this period was usually drawn differently.

As we can see, the hieratic chisel sign (fig. 12.2) used by the builders of Menkaure's pyramid complex some fifty or so years *after* the Great Pyramid is a chisel sign that actually does look pretty much like a chisel, and this hieratic form of the sign is actually not too far removed or evolved from the original monumental hieroglyphic form. It is also worth mentioning that the chisel sign found at Menkaure's pyramid complex is preceded by the mouth sign (fig. 12.2). In ancient Egyptian writing the chisel and mouth signs often (though not always) were written together. This is because the chisel sign can have two different phonetic sounds, and the mouth sign, when used in this way, is known as a phonetic complement as it helps the reader to differentiate one phonetic interpretation from the other. The disputed *q* sign in the Great Pyramid is believed by Egyptologists to have the same phonetic sound as the chisel sign that is normally presented alongside the mouth sign, except, on this occasion, there is no mouth sign; no phonetic complement is present.

Why, then, do we find in Khufu's pyramid what is believed by Egyptologists to be a chisel sign that is quite unlike the hieratic chisel sign that the ancient Egyptians apparently used both *before* and *after* Khufu's time? Is the absence of the mouth sign (phonetic complement)

Exhibit 8 • Signs Out of Time 149

perhaps an indication that this sign has been incorrectly identified?

Alas, with ancient Egyptian writing nothing is ever simple. As noted in chapter 1, ancient Egyptian writing made with ink or paint (as opposed to the sculpted monumental script) slowly evolved over time to morph, stylistically, into very different signs—simplified hieratic signs—that represented particular monumental hieroglyphic signs. And although some hieratic signs existed prior to the sculpted hieroglyphs, according to Hans Goedicke it seems that the simplified forms of signs became standard only from around the Fifth Dynasty.[1]

And so, it is argued, the chisel sign in the Khufu gang name (fig. 12.1) is simply an evolved and simplified hieratic version of the monumental hieroglyphic chisel sign. This implies, of course, that the gangs of Menkaure's pyramid-building project, built long *after* Khufu's pyramid, for some reason reverted back to using the least evolved hieratic chisel sign (fig. 12.2) to make their own graffiti marks on the stone blocks of Menkaure's pyramid complex—a kind of reverse evolution.

In his standard reference of hieratic signs, *Old Hieratic Paleography,* Goedicke shows that the closest match to the hieratic chisel sign we observe in Campbell's Chamber (fig. 12.1) arises in the paleographical record sometime between Dynasties Eight and Eleven,[2] long after the Great Pyramid and its internal relief chambers were built and sealed. So it seems that this chisel sign (if that is what it is) found its way into the Great Pyramid long before it had actually evolved into the form we find in the pyramid.

If we now consider some of the other signs in the various gang names from these relief chambers, strangely, we find a similar pattern—signs that, according to Goedicke's *Old Hieratic Paleography*, have their closest hieratic match also arising sometime between Dynasties Eight and Eleven.

The hieratic signs shown in figure 12.3 (p. 150) represent (from left): Sail,[3] Quail,[4] and Sekhem Sceptre.[5] Once again, consulting Goedicke's *Old Hieratic Paleography,* we find that these signs have their closest hieratic match arising sometime between the Eighth and Eleventh Dynasties, long after the Great Pyramid was completed.

Most of the other signs within the gang names of the relief chambers

Fig. 12.3. These signs from the various gang names found in the relief chambers of the Great Pyramid find their closest paleographical hieratic matches sometime between the Eighth and Eleventh Dynasties. (Image: Scott Creighton)

(for which we have sufficient data) appear to have changed very little up to the end of the Eleventh Dynasty (some a little earlier). For example, the folded cloth sign (fig. 12.4, *far right*) barely evolved at all across all of this time, about one thousand years of ancient Egyptian history. What this means, of course, is that the hieratic signs in these gang names (for which there is sufficient data to check) were being used between Dynasties Eight and Eleven, which raises an interesting possibility: Could it be that around this time of ancient Egyptian history there was some form of restoration project occurring at Giza? Is this perhaps the reason that we find gang names (perhaps from a Khufu revival cult) using hieratic signs from this much later period and why the signs have been written horizontally rather than the much earlier vertical arrangement? And could it have been that Vyse came across this cache of gang names somewhere at Giza, recognized the Khufu cartouche, and simply had everything copied into the relief chambers, not realizing, in his ignorance of evolving hieratic texts, that he was copying hieratic signs from much later dynasties?

ANOTHER SIGN?

As stated earlier, the chisel sign in the Khufu gang name is disputed among Egyptologists. So, if not a hieratic chisel sign, then what other character might this crudely drawn sign in the gang name of Khufu

Exhibit 8 • Signs Out of Time 151

Fig. 12.4. Artist's impression of facsimile drawing of the Khufu gang name (without the cartouche) from Campbell's Chamber (Image: Scott Creighton, based on original drawing by J. R. Hill)

actually be? A possible clue to this comes to us from the facsimile drawing Vyse had his assistant Hill make of this gang name (fig. 12.4).

Putting aside the anomalous orientation of these glyphs relative to Hill's signature (which, as previously noted, uniquely among Hill's facsimiles, locks them wrongly into a horizontal arrangement), at first glance there does not appear to be anything remarkable or unusual about this drawing of the gang name signs. However, a closer inspection of this facsimile sheet in the British Museum reveals something rather curious.

Notice that at the bottom right-hand corner of the facsimile sheet (fig. 12.4) a small symbol has been drawn that is similar (though inverted) to the stafflike sign to the far right of the gang name. This small mark was made in black ink, ink not unlike that used by Vyse in his private notes.

We have to ask, Why has this small stafflike hieratic sign been drawn in black ink on this facsimile sheet of the Khufu gang name? Of the twenty-eight facsimile drawings made by Hill, *only* this single drawing bears a small hieratic mark drawn in black ink. So, what is it about this particular drawing that might have brought this small stafflike sign to have been placed in the bottom-right corner of the sheet? What is its purpose?

This curious mark almost seems like an afterthought, as though it has been placed on this drawing as a reminder of something. Could this "something" perhaps be a modified sign? In other words, is it possible that the questionable chisel glyph we observe today in Campbell's Chamber was actually meant to be something else (i.e., a second stafflike glyph) but that, by accident or design, it was "wrongly" copied (by Hill) onto the wall of Campbell's Chamber, thereby creating the dubious and contentious chisel sign on the roof of the chamber? Could it be that the sign Hill *meant* to copy onto the ceiling block of Campbell's Chamber (from the secret cache) was actually a second stafflike glyph but that, for whatever reason, he messed up in copying it onto the gabled roof? And, having messed it up (by mistake or by intention), did he then copy this "mistake" onto his facsimile drawing, perhaps making sure, of course, to record the *intended* sign by placing a small, surreptitious note of it in black ink at the bottom-right corner of the sheet?

But what, if anything, is there to support such a contention? Well, the first thing to say is that it is unlikely that Hill would mess up such a glyph in several different ways. If he messed up this glyph when painting it onto the roof gable of Campbell's Chamber, then it is likely that he simply messed up one aspect of the sign; that is, the handle loop, which he should have painted similarly to the stafflike glyph to its immediate right (fig. 12.4). This means, of course, that the small horizontal stroke on the shaft of the sign was probably *not* a mistake and that this small stroke was actually part of the original stafflike sign Hill attempted to copy. This means that there would be two slightly different stafflike signs—one *with* a small horizontal stroke on the shaft and one without. But was such a sign (i.e., a staff with a small horizontal stroke on the shaft) extant at this time in ancient Egypt?

As it happens, we find that this sign appears among some graffiti painted by work gangs at the Fourth Dynasty harbor of Wadi al-Jarf (fig. 12.5).

As we can see, the graffiti from the harbor of Wadi al-Jarf presents a painted stafflike sign that has a small, horizontal stroke projecting from the vertical shaft of the sign. So clearly this variation of the stafflike sign *does* exist elsewhere in the archaeological record. But what evidence is

Exhibit 8 • Signs Out of Time 153

there that might indicate that Hill's original source was, in fact, a staff-like glyph with a small horizontal stroke on the vertical shaft, that this is what he *should* have copied onto the gabled roof trussing of Campbell's Chamber, but that he messed up? The proof of this can actually be found not in Vyse's *published* account but in his *private* field notes.

In his entry of June 16, 1837, Vyse drew the hieratic signs for the Khufu gang name into his private journal (fig. 12.6). As we can see in figure 12.6, in Vyse's *private* journal we do not have the hieratic chisel glyph that can be seen today in the gang name in Campbell's Chamber

Fig. 12.5. Reproduction of Khnum-Khuf gang name from harbor graffiti at Wadi al-Jarf showing a stafflike glyph with a small horizontal stroke on the shaft (left column, middle glyph) (Image: Scott Creighton)

Fig. 12.6. Reproduction of the Khufu gang name (without the cartouche) from Vyse's private journal showing the stafflike glyph with a small horizontal stroke on the shaft (third from left) (Image: Scott Creighton)

but rather a second stafflike glyph with a small horizontal stroke, just like that found among the graffiti at the harbor of Wadi al-Jarf (fig. 12.5). Here, then, we may be observing in Vyse's private notes the sign that Hill *should* have copied into the Great Pyramid but that, by accident or intent, was "modified" by him.

It seems, then, that while Vyse may have correctly recorded the original source into his private journal, Hill subsequently copied it incorrectly onto the gabled roof. By so doing he inadvertently created a sign that, though not perfect in every detail, closely resembled the ancient Egyptian hieratic chisel sign, so much so that Egyptologists, even though some disagree, by and large believe the sign was intended as a hieratic chisel sign, even if roughly drawn.

But, as we have seen, the actual truth of the matter is revealed in Vyse's private journal, that this sign was originally a stafflike sign (with a small horizontal stroke on the shaft) like the one attested at Wadi al-Jarf. We have one sign written in Vyse's private journal but an entirely different sign in the actual chamber. Why the contradiction?

So, once again, with this contradictory evidence from Vyse's private journal we have reason to doubt the accepted version of the discovery of the markings in these chambers as presented by him in his published account.

Of course, skeptics will assert that Vyse (rather than Hill) merely miscopied the gang name from Campbell's Chamber into his private journal. While this remains possible, it would require Vyse to have miscopied a sign from Campbell's Chamber (a sign that Egyptologists themselves do not entirely agree on), a sign of which there is no other example in this period outside this chamber, and to then somehow manage to substitute it in his private notes with the variant of a sign that actually *is* evidenced elsewhere in this period. It also requires us to accept that the ancient builders, apparently having been using the questionable hieratic chisel sign we observe in Khufu's pyramid, reverted back to using the less-evolved hieratic chisel sign (fig. 12.2) long after the Great Pyramid was built, as evidenced by the graffiti found in Menkaure's pyramid complex. This makes little sense.

It seems that the more likely scenario here is that the two stafflike

Exhibit 8 • Signs Out of Time 155

signs in Vyse's private journal were true and correct copies of marks Vyse found elsewhere (his master source) and that Vyse had Hill copy this source into the pyramid, whereupon one of the two stafflike signs (i.e., the sign with the horizontal stroke) was miscopied, either by mistake or by design. And, as previously stated, this badly copied stafflike sign may explain why we now find the small, curious stafflike sign drawn in black ink at the bottom-right corner of Hill's facsimile drawing (fig. 12.4)—as if someone was surreptitiously noting what the disputed chisel sign *should* have been (i.e., the stafflike sign we find in Vyse's private journal).

THE TWO STAFFS

One other aspect of this curious situation that also needs to be considered is the meaning of the word (the gang name) when it has two stafflike signs instead of what is believed to be a chisel sign beside a stafflike sign. After all, if the word with two stafflike signs was entirely meaningless, then that would suggest that Vyse had copied the gang name incorrectly into his private journal. So, what meaning, if any, does the gang name have when it is written with two stafflike signs?

We learned earlier that the Khufu gang name in Campbell's Chamber of the Great Pyramid (fig. 12.1) has been interpreted by Egyptologists as meaning "friends" or "companions" of Khufu. However, when we replace the disputed chisel sign with a second stafflike sign, as shown in Vyse's private notes (fig. 12.6), the meaning changes very significantly. Instead of being interpreted as meaning "friends" or "companions," the gang name written with two stafflike signs now becomes "destroyers" or "burners" (of Khufu), a very profound change indeed. And it is a change that may actually have more historical merit and significance than the mainstream interpretation.

Very few things about the life of Khufu have come down to us from the writings of the ancient historians. But one of the things that we are told about Khufu, courtesy of Herodotus, is that he was apparently utterly despised by the entire population of the country as a cruel leader who closed all the temples and forced his people into terrible hardships through the construction of his pyramid. Indeed, Khufu was so despised by the population that it is said that he could not even use his pyramid for his burial for fear of it being ransacked and his remains destroyed, his afterlife terminated before it had even begun.

We have to ask, then, What makes more sense given what we understand about the type of ruler Khufu apparently was? Is it more likely that we would find an inscription with "friends" (of Khufu) or one that reads "destroyers" (of Khufu)?

CHAPTER TWELVE SUMMARY

- The gang name associated with the Khufu cartouche is commonly translated as "friends" or "companions" (of Khufu).
- The hieratic chisel sign within the Khufu gang name in Campbell's Chamber is somewhat curious, having a directly comparable hieratic sign only from a much later period.
- Several other signs from the various gang names present in the Great Pyramid find their closest hieratic match in the paleographical record sometime between the Eighth and Eleventh Dynasties, long after the pyramid was built and its internal chambers sealed.
- The gangs in the *later* construction of Menkaure's pyramid complex used a hieratic chisel sign that had barely evolved from the original monumental hieroglyphic sign. Thus we have in Khufu's pyramid a supposed hieratic chisel sign that had evolved quite considerably from the original monumental hieroglyphic sign and a *later* chisel sign from Menkaure's complex that shows the hieratic chisel sign in this period having barely evolved at all from the original monumental hieroglyphic sign.
- The chisel sign is usually (though not always) accompanied with the mouth sign.
- Hill's facsimile drawing of the Khufu gang name shows in the bottom-right corner of the facsimile sheet a small stafflike sign drawn in black ink.
- Of Hill's twenty-eight facsimile drawings, this is the only one with such a small hieratic sign drawn in black ink. It may have been placed on this sheet to indicate the sign Hill had *meant* to paint.

Exhibit 8 • Signs Out of Time 157

- There is hieroglyphic evidence from Wadi al-Jarf of a variant staff-like sign with a small horizontal stroke on the vertical shaft.
- Vyse's *private* journal shows the Khufu gang name written with *two* stafflike signs (one with a horizontal stroke on the shaft) and no chisel sign.
- Herodotus tells us that Khufu was a king who was highly despised by the entire ancient Egyptian population, so much so, in fact, that Herodotus tells us Khufu did not have himself interred in his pyramid, so afraid was he that the population would desecrate his remains. A gang name with two stafflike signs would be interpreted as "destroyers" or "burners" (of Khufu).

13

EXHIBIT 9

THE JOURNAL SPEAKS

In the absence of official scientific data proving the authenticity of the painted hieratic signs within the Great Pyramid, it seemed that the only remaining avenue to explore that might allow us to perhaps determine the truth of these marks was Vyse's *private* journal—his personal field notes—from his time at Giza in 1837. While Vyse tells us much about his activities at Giza in his *published* account, it was possible that if his private field notes could be located and examined, then there may be more to be gleaned from those pages—information that Vyse would have much preferred not to have in the public domain.

Author Alan Alford had long sought this document, as he too realized that if it could be located and inspected, it might reveal some pertinent truths about Vyse's time at Giza that had been omitted by Vyse from his published work. For myself, I felt that if Vyse's private journal could be found and examined, then the truth of Walter Allen's logbook account regarding the story passed down by his great-grandfather Humphries Brewer might be found somewhere in its pages, that we might find the truth of a story that seems to have been entirely expunged in Vyse's "official" account of his operations at Giza.

In short, if Brewer *had* been with Vyse in Egypt in 1837, as Allen's logbook tells us, then it was perhaps possible that Vyse, although having eradicated all traces of Brewer's presence from his published account (as a result of their dispute) may have left entries of Brewer's name and

Exhibit 9 • The Journal Speaks   159

activities in his private journal. This was my thinking, and if it turned out to be correct, then it might at least offer a means to corroborate Allen's controversial logbook entry from 1954 that indicated a fraud having been perpetrated by Raven and Hill.

So, in March 2014, I set about looking for Vyse's private journal, his field notes written during his operations at Giza. Thanks to the Internet, it did not take very long to locate the document. Over the years I had halfheartedly searched for this document but had always come up empty-handed (as had Alford). On this occasion the where-abouts of this nearly 180-year-old private journal presented itself: the Centre for Buckinghamshire Studies in Aylesbury, England (fig. 13.1), about four hundred miles from my home in Glasgow. So my wife, Louise, and I would have to drive a round trip of eight hundred miles (1,288 kilometers) to have a look at Vyse's archive.

We set off on a beautiful spring morning, full of excitement at the little adventure that lay before us, not knowing where it would take us or, indeed, if we would find anything at all of any great relevance to our quest. However, when we finally arrived at the archive center we were not to be disappointed, finding in Vyse's private notes much more than we had ever bargained for.

Vyse's private handwritten journal consists of around six hundred

Fig. 13.1. Logo for the Centre for Buckinghamshire Studies, Aylesbury, England, where Vyse's private journal is held in the family archive (Image: Scott Creighton)

pages of yellowing, folded foolscap pages (written on both sides), tied together in a bundle with a thin white ribbon and all contained within two rather unremarkable card folders. Although the ink on some of the pages is perfectly clear, on many others it is exceedingly faint, browning with age. On many pages the ink from the reverse side of the thin paper would "ghost" through the page, making it somewhat difficult to read. But this was the least of our problems with the document, as a quick perusal of some of the tattered, dog-eared pages would soon prove.

Vyse's handwriting is almost impossible to read, a scrawling, erratic script where many words are contracted or expanded and where the same letter can often take a quite different form depending on where it appears in a particular word or sentence, and on occasion, some of his words would be abbreviated. And this is to say nothing about a number of his words being quite archaic and rarely used in modern English. I had experienced doctor's prescriptions that were far easier to read than Vyse's execrable pages. It is also worth mentioning here that every single page—all six hundred or so of them—bears a long vertical line running from top to bottom through the middle of the page, as have many of the drawings made by Vyse. One can only presume that these "strike-through" marks were created some years later when Vyse was using his handwritten journal as source material while writing his books.

In consideration of these difficulties, we sought permission from the library to take digital photographs of the journal pages so that Louise and I could take them home and analyze them at our leisure. Fortunately this wasn't a problem (so long as we didn't use flash photography).

So, for the next two days, Louise and I set about the not insignificant task of photographing each and every page of Vyse's handwritten journal, along with some other material in his archive, which included some family letters. The sheer magnitude of the task wasn't lost on us, and we quickly realized that finding anything significant within these intractably obscure pages could take months, if not years. (Indeed, a clear reference to the name Brewer has not, as yet, been found in Vyse's private journal, although a few possible occurrences that may very well be the name Brewer have been identified, but at the time of this writing, they have not been confirmed by handwriting experts.) It didn't help

Exhibit 9 • The Journal Speaks   161

our task, either, that upon returning home we discovered that a sizeable number of our photographic images were of insufficient quality to make a proper analysis.

But massive as this undertaking was, it always seems to be the case that just when your research seems to have hit the buffers, the "library angel" appears and hands to you exactly what you need, just when you need it—which turned out to be the case here. The gods of serendipity appeared to be on our side.

MORE CARTOUCHE ANOMALIES

Hour after hour we had been turning and photographing the delicate pages, seeing nothing before us but an endless, virtually meaningless scrawl. But then, as Louise turned one of the pages for me to photograph, I noticed that it had some hieroglyphs written on it. Very few pages had such content, so these markings easily caught the eye. But these weren't just any old hieroglyphic marks that Vyse had written on this page; it was the *cartouche of Suphis/Khufu.*

Resting the camera on the table, I took a closer look at the cartouche that Vyse had drawn on the page. Although drawn fairly small, it was clear enough to see that there was something odd about its composition, which I pointed out to Louise; she agreed. We continued photographing the dog-eared pages, and several pages farther on we found a *second* Suphis/Khufu cartouche drawn by Vyse, and just like the first cartouche that we had found earlier, there was something very peculiar about its composition. Both of the cartouches drawn by Vyse in his private journal were different in a very subtle but highly significant way from the actual cartouche we find painted on the gabled roof of Campbell's Chamber. There was something clearly *missing* in both renderings of the cartouche in Vyse's private journal, something that is clearly *not* missing from the actual cartouche that these two cartouche drawings in his private diary were supposedly copied from.

Louise and I looked at each other in stunned silence as the realization and enormity of what we had found gradually sunk in, for before us, on these two pages in Vyse's private journal, was compelling evidence that the cartouche of Suphis/Khufu must, in fact, have been forged by him—just as a number of researchers and writers over the years had suspected. To say that we were dumbstruck by what we had uncovered would be an understatement; here we had found in the colonel's own diary, in his own hand, evidence that proved, beyond reasonable doubt, that Vyse had perpetrated the hoax of all history.

Having returned to our hotel late that evening, not a little exhausted from our day's efforts, we sat and stared in bemused silence at the two digital pages on our laptop screens, struggling to wrap our minds around their game-changing implications. The irony of what we had found was not lost on us. Here we were, barely able to read a few words of Vyse's early nineteenth-century handwriting, yet the ancient Egyptian hieroglyphics, which he had so meticulously copied into his private journal, revealed to us the truth of the disputed inscriptions in the Great Pyramid, a truth that many have been seeking for decades, if not longer—that they had been faked.

JOURNAL ENTRY, MAY 27, 1837

On May 27, 1837, Vyse and his team finally managed to blast their way into the final relieving chamber of the Great Pyramid, which Vyse had already named Campbell's Chamber in honor of the British consul to Egypt, Colonel Patrick Campbell. In his journal entry of that day, Vyse drew the cartouche of Khufu (fig. 13.2).

Fig. 13.2. Artist's impression of Khufu cartouche (enlarged) presented in Vyse's private journal entry of May 27, 1837 (Image: Scott Creighton, based on original by Colonel Vyse)

Exhibit 9 • The Journal Speaks   163

Around this cartouche Vyse wrote a highly incriminating piece of text, which will be presented later in this chapter. For the moment, however, concentrating on the cartouche itself we observe a very odd anomaly: the disc within the cartouche (fig. 13.2, *far right*) presents two small dots side by side where there should, in fact, be three stacked horizontal lines. The two small dots under the snake or horned viper sign attest to this being the cartouche (ostensibly) from Campbell's Chamber, as does the text Vyse wrote around this cartouche.

The disc within the cartouche drawn on this page is categorically *not* the same disc that we observe within the *actual* cartouche we find in Campbell's Chamber today. Why Vyse would not have placed three stacked lines within the disc is a complete mystery, especially so when we consider the appearance of his *second* private journal drawing of the Suphis/Khufu cartouche in Campbell's Chamber, made just more than two weeks later on June 16, 1837. In his second rendering of the Khufu cartouche Vyse now draws the cartouche disc entirely devoid of *any* internal markings—no parallel dots or stacked horizontal lines, just a plain, blank disc (fig. 13.3).

In this journal entry of June 16, 1837, Vyse drew a couple of other Khufu cartouches in the margin at the foot of this page, which we will consider shortly. As we can see in figure 13.3, Vyse makes a small note to the right of this cartouche that reads "in Campbell's Chamber." There can be no mistake; this cartouche, now with just a *blank* disc, is what Vyse in June 1837 states was present at that time in Campbell's

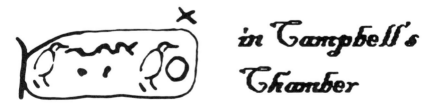

Fig. 13.3. Artist's impression of Khufu cartouche (enlarged) with text as presented in Vyse's private journal entry of June 16, 1837 (mid page). Note that the disc within the cartouche is entirely devoid of the stacked horizontal lines; it is blank. Vyse notes to the right of this cartouche "in Campbell's Chamber." (Image: Scott Creighton, based on original by Colonel Vyse)

Chamber. As is easily observed, the disc within the cartouche of this drawing of June 16 clearly differs from Vyse's earlier drawing of May 27, which presented two small dots within the disc, while *both* drawings clearly differ to what we *presently* find in the chamber, which is a disc with three stacked horizontal lines.

How can this be?

It is perhaps worth noting here that the cartouche disc with the two small dots (fig. 13.2) might have resulted from ink droplets inadvertently spilling from Vyse's fountain pen into the disc. Another possibility to explain these dots may be related to the positioning of this cartouche graphic, which has been written right on the fold of the page. Though it is not shown in figure 13.2 (for the purposes of clarity), this cartouche has been struck through by Vyse with a fountain pen (fig. 13.14), like almost all other graphics in his private journal. It is possible that having struck through the page with a vertical line and then likewise the cartouche graphic, Vyse then simply folded the page, thereby causing small ink spots from his editing strike-through process to transfer elsewhere onto the page (i.e., into the area of the cartouche disc).

Having analyzed the position of all of these inked lines, it seems quite possible that this is how these two small dots of ink may have found their way into the cartouche disc on this page. In other words, it is quite probable that Vyse had originally drawn the cartouche disc of May 27 not with two small dots at all but rather with a blank disc, just like the blank disc he drew in the later cartouche disc of June 16. However, regardless of the actual truth of this, what is perfectly clear is that Vyse, on *two* quite separate occasions, did not copy the Khufu cartouche disc into his private journal as it actually appears today in Campbell's Chamber—a strange anomaly indeed, and one that surely demands an explanation.

JOURNAL ENTRY, JUNE 16, 1837

Let us now turn our attention to Vyse's private journal entry of June 16, 1837, which, as we will see, reveals other highly incriminating evi-

Exhibit 9 • The Journal Speaks 165

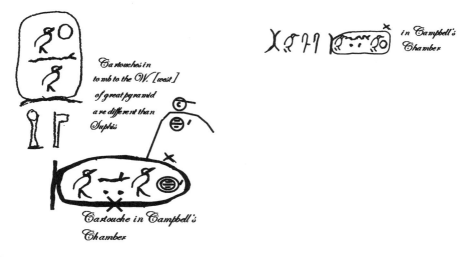

Fig.13.4. Artist's impression of Vyse journal entry of June 16, 1837. (Only the relevant information is presented here. There is much more text on the original page of Vyse's journal than is shown in this reproduction.) Note that in the original graphic in the journal the Khufu cartouche (top right) has a single diagonal editing stroke through it (as have all the journal graphics), which, in the interests of clarity, has not been reproduced here. (Image: Scott Creighton, based on original by Colonel Vyse)

dence pointing to fraudulent activity. Figure 13.4 reproduces an artist's impression of the relevant page from Vyse's private journal.

This entry from Vyse's private journal contains a number of odd and curious features. We see that the colonel has drawn a number of different circles with curious marks beside them; he has scored some things out, has placed an *X* in several locations, and has made a number of small horizontal and vertical strokes. We notice also that there are four circles drawn on the page that have just a *single* circle outline, whereas the circle in the Khufu cartouche at the foot of the page (in the bottom-left margin of Vyse's journal) is the only circle that has a *double* outline (i.e., a circle within a circle), see figure 13.5 on page 166.

But, as noted above, the most striking anomaly immediately observed on this page is the Khufu cartouche at the top right. The disc within this cartouche is entirely devoid of the stacked horizontal lines

Cartouche in Campbell's Chamber

Fig. 13.5. Artist's impression of Khufu cartouche as presented in Vyse's private journal entry of June 16, 1837, at the foot of the page. Note that the disc in this cartouche has three small, stacked horizontal lines. Vyse writes below this drawing, "Cartouche in Campbell's Chamber." (Image: Scott Creighton, based on original drawing by Colonel Vyse)

that we see in the cartouche disc at the foot of the same page (and in the cartouche that we actually find in the chamber today, which carries the three stacked lines within the disc).

With these two slightly different cartouche images on this same page of Vyse's private journal, we are presented with a clear contradiction. As noted above, beside the Khufu cartouche with the *blank* disc (fig. 13.4, *top right*) Vyse writes alongside, "in Campbell's Chamber," and then below the cartouche with the *striated* disc (fig. 13.4, *bottom left*), he also writes, "Cartouche in Campbell's Chamber."

So what is going on here? How are we to make sense of this? Given that there is only *one* cartouche of Suphis/Khufu in Campbell's Chamber presenting a disc, how can Vyse write in his journal that *both* of these slightly different cartouches are present in the chamber (i.e., a cartouche with a blank disc *and* a cartouche with a striated disc)? And what on earth are we to make of all the peculiar marks we see in this journal entry? In short, why would Vyse draw the Suphis/Khufu cartouche in his journal, on two separate occasions, differently from what we actually observe today in this chamber?

Exhibit 9 • The Journal Speaks 167

A number of possible reasons have been proposed to try to explain this anomaly. Perhaps Vyse simply did not observe the stacked horizontal lines in the disc when he first observed the Suphis/Khufu cartouche in the chamber on May 27, 1837, especially since he would only have had light from a candle or an oil lamp. While this is possible, it seems highly unlikely for a number of reasons.

1. Vyse states quite categorically in his published book that Campbell's Chamber, in which the Suphis/Khufu cartouche was found, was "minutely examined" for marks. If the chamber was minutely examined, then it seems unlikely that Vyse would have missed these marks within the cartouche disc.

2. Vyse manages to observe the two small dots under the snake sign of the cartouche, so one must presume that having observed this very small detail (perhaps using only a candle or oil lamp), he would have easily observed the much larger and more prominent lines within the disc.

3. Vyse, by this time in his operations, had already blasted his way into three other chambers below Campbell's Chamber, and in those other chambers he found several cartouches of Khnum-Khuf (Khufu's full name), *all* of which presented a disc with center marks of some kind and all of which were meticulously recorded by Hill in his facsimile drawings. As such, when Vyse finally opened Campbell's Chamber (the highest and last chamber), his previous experience from the chambers below would surely have had him fully anticipating finding the Khufu cartouche disc with similar center markings—dots, lines, or whatever. Given his experience of the other cartouche discs with center markings found in the chambers below, finding the Khufu disc entirely devoid of any marks would most surely have piqued Vyse's curiosity, and he would most certainly have had it double-checked.

4. As we have previously noted, there were *two* such Khufu cartouches drawn by Vyse in his private journal—one entry on May 27 and another on June 16, 1837—both *without* the stacked

lines. Are we to believe that Vyse wrongly copied this cartouche disc on *both* occasions? Furthermore, on May 30, Vyse's assistant Hill was tasked by Vyse to make a facsimile copy of the Khufu cartouche in Campbell's Chamber. Hill's drawing (which I viewed in the British Museum) most certainly contains the three lines in the cartouche disc, yet on June 16 (more than two weeks *after* Hill's drawing had been completed) Vyse *again* enters the Khufu cartouche into his journal with just a plain disc. Why did Vyse make a "mistake" and then repeat the same mistake even though Hill's facsimile would (presumably by this time) have shown him the correct spelling (i.e., a disc with three internal stacked lines)? Was Hill's drawing of the Khufu cartouche disc, at this time, *also* devoid of the three stacked lines?

Perhaps, as some have further suggested, Vyse was merely making a rough note of the cartouche in his journal, perhaps making the disc too small for him to be able to insert the three stacked horizontal lines. Again this proposal, while possible, is highly unlikely for the following reasons.

1. As previously noted above, Vyse was detailed and meticulous enough to draw the two small dots under the snake glyph (which are actually a mistake and not part of Khufu's name). If this was merely a rough drawing, as some have suggested, why would Vyse be so meticulous in his recording of this tiny detail under the snake sign on two occasions and then be so casual and fail to record the much more obvious detail within the disc sign on two occasions? That makes little sense.

2. Vyse would have been fully aware that he would be using his written journal (including the various drawings he made therein) as the basis from which he would write and publish his future book of his operations at Giza. As such, accuracy in recording these markings would have been of paramount importance to him, and such detail would naturally have been crucial to that accuracy—especially so given that Vyse was in no way a specialist in this field.

Exhibit 9 • The Journal Speaks 169

3. Failing to accurately copy fairly obvious details from the cartouche of a king could have caused serious interpretative consequences for scholars back in London, and Vyse would almost certainly have understood that. He would be unlikely to have a second chance at this; it would have been imperative to accurately copy the detail of these markings, particularly the cartouches, correctly the first time and to ensure that his own renderings were consistent with and corroborated those of Mr. Hill to prevent any confusion afterward.

4. While it is true that the two Khufu cartouche discs drawn by Vyse on May 27 and June 16 are very small, and, as such, it would have made it difficult to clearly present three stacked horizontal lines within them, it is equally possible that these two discs were rendered in this small size simply because Vyse had no intention of inserting any stacked lines within either of the two cartouche discs because the horizontal lines simply did not exist in his master source. An analysis of these discs on the relevant pages of Vyse's private journal shows that there was sufficient space on each page for Vyse to have drawn a much larger cartouche and/or disc into which he could have easily placed three stacked lines. That he didn't use the available space on the page to draw a larger disc to accommodate stacked lines suggests that there were no such lines to be accommodated, hence that is why he drew the smaller blank disc.

5. If this was merely a rough drawing of the cartouche Vyse was jotting into his journal and of no real importance to him, why then would he place a corrective mark (the small X sign) above the blank discs to indicate that the discs had been wrongly copied? Indeed, why place an X mark here at all? Surely it would have been more natural to *correct* the perceived "mistake" either by placing the missing lines into the existing blank disc or by drawing another disc (with stacked lines) in place of the X mark? This odd edit mark seems more indicative of Vyse having copied this disc *correctly* (i.e., with no striations) from his secret source (hence his reluctance to actually change it here) but now,

having found other examples of the Khufu disc *with* the horizontal lines, believes his original source to be wrong or incomplete, thus the simple X marks to indicate such.

In short, it would have been vital to Vyse that all of these inscriptions were copied as accurately as possible by himself, Hill, and Perring. Indeed, the importance Vyse placed on this accuracy could not be more clearly demonstrated than by his seeking of a number of independent eyewitnesses (including Sir Robert Arbuthnot, Joseph Cartwright Brettell, and Henry Raven) to attest to the accuracy of many of Hill's facsimile drawings, although, curiously, only Hill himself attested to the accuracy of the Suphis/Khufu gang name drawings. Bizarrely, not even Vyse added his signature to verify the likeness of these particular facsimiles made by Hill.

The simple truth of all of this may well be that when Vyse and his closest assistants first entered Campbell's Chamber there was no Khufu cartouche present at all (nor any Khnum-Khuf cartouches in the lower chambers). *Some* glyphs may well have been present (as the eyewitness account of Walter Allen's great-grandfather seems to suggest) but not the gang names bearing the royal inscriptions. From what we have learned of events elsewhere in this book, it seems that Vyse and his closest confidants placed these various gang names into these chambers themselves, copied from a master source they had found elsewhere outside the pyramid, a source that—fatefully—presented the Khufu cartouche with just a plain blank disc, which is why Vyse presented the cartouche disc from Campbell's Chamber without any horizontal lines (on two occasions) in his private journal.

But something was about to change in Vyse's thinking, and it is something that explains the contradiction we find in his private journal entry of June 16; that is, how the one Suphis/Khufu cartouche in Campbell's Chamber could have both a blank disc *and* a striated disc at the same time. It seems that around this time Vyse had a change of mind and slightly modified the hitherto blank disc he had placed in Campbell's Chamber by adding to it the three stacked, horizontal lines. This change appears to have been prompted by some new critical

Exhibit 9 • The Journal Speaks   171

information he had received earlier in June from one of his assistants, Perring.

THE TWO SPELLINGS OF SUPHIS

The crucial point to understand here is that *both* these spellings of the Suphis/Khufu name present in Vyse's journal entry of June 16 are, in fact, *correct*. This is to say that, according to mainstream Egyptology, the name Khufu can be written with either a striated disc with any number of stacked horizontal (or even diagonal) striations *or* with just a plain blank disc. Indeed, numerous examples of these various spellings exist in the archaeological record, which probably explains why Vyse originally believed the Khufu/Suphis name should be spelled with just a *blank* disc, for that is probably how the disc in the Suphis/Khufu cartouche in his master source appeared (although the Khnum-Khuf examples would have had internal markings within the disc).

However, in 1837 this fact wasn't yet fully understood, and when Perring presented to Vyse (on June 2) information that showed a slightly different spelling of Suphis/Khufu (i.e., a cartouche disc that wasn't blank but contained three horizontal lines), this new information created an ambiguity and caused Vyse to have doubts over which was the correct disc to use; he wouldn't have known then what we know today, that a blank disc is just as acceptable for the spelling of Khufu as a disc containing striations. This doubt is clearly expressed in Vyse's June 16 journal entry, where a series of edits and annotations are clearly observed on this page.

Vyse would have well understood that if he had sent a facsimile copy of the Khufu cartouche back to London with what turned out to be the incorrect spelling, he could have been very quickly uncovered as a fraudster and his "discoveries" consigned to ignominy. There was much at stake here. If he could just be the first to empirically connect the Great Pyramid to Suphis/Khufu, then his name would be immortalized in history. He had to get the Khufu cartouche right. Should the disc be blank, or should it have internal lines like those in the Khnum-Khuf cartouche (the full name of Khufu)?

The fact that the plain-disc version of the Khufu cartouche and the striated-disc version *both* exist in the archaeological record leads us, as previously stated, to an intriguing possibility: Might it be that Vyse originally found an example of a Khufu cartouche (his master source) with just the *plain* disc, which he copied into his journal (and presumably the Great Pyramid), believing this version of the Khufu cartouche to be the *only* (thus correct) spelling of the king's name? And did Vyse discover some time later that, in fact, there were examples of the Khufu cartouche with striated discs, leading him to believe (wrongly) that the plain disc version he had originally found (and had placed in the Great Pyramid) was perhaps a disc that was *unfinished* by the ancient Egyptian scribe who originally created it and that to render the Khufu name fully and correctly required the plain disc to be completed by adding horizontal striations? There is some compelling evidence from Vyse's journal that this may well have been his thinking.

As can be seen in his private journal entry of June 16, Vyse has drawn one vertical Suphis/Khufu cartouche with a blank disc (fig. 13.4, *top left*) and also *two* horizontal Suphis/Khufu cartouches, *both* of which he states are from Campbell's Chamber, yet they each have a slightly different disc within the cartouche.

However, because we know there is only *one* complete Khufu cartouche in Campbell's Chamber, both discs on this journal page cannot be right. So it is here, in his private journal, that we find the very essence of Vyse's doubt, his contradiction, and his deliberation; here on this journal page we observe Vyse contemplating a necessary change to what he once believed was the correct spelling of Khufu. The original plain-disc version of the cartouche that he had written twice into his diary and had copied into the Great Pyramid actually required three horizontal lines to be added—or so it seems he believed. It is right here on this page of Vyse's private journal that we find the evidence that lays bare the hoax of all history.

Why should Vyse be having such deliberations at all—and why now? It was not Vyse's job to try to interpret the painted marks that he supposedly found in these chambers; that was the job of the experts back in London. Vyse's responsibility was to explore and record any

Exhibit 9 • The Journal Speaks   173

important findings. This controversial diary entry had been made some three weeks *after* Vyse had opened and entered Campbell's Chamber. What was it that had occurred to bring Vyse to revisit the cartouche in the Great Pyramid weeks after its supposed discovery? Why was he suddenly starting to question the spelling of this cartouche? A clue is given in the journal entry of June 16 when Vyse writes:

Cartouches in tomb to the W. [west] of Great Pyramid are different than Suphis.[1]

The above comment made by Vyse imparts to us two very important pieces of information.

1. Clearly from this comment we can logically deduce that Vyse already knew (or *believed* he knew) how the Suphis/Khufu cartouche *should* be written, because he could recognize ones that were different from it, and that he knew this information long before Hill's facsimile drawing of it had been sent to the experts back in London for verification of the Suphis/Khufu name.
2. At the same time, Vyse had realized some Khufu cartouches were spelled slightly differently (with lines in the disc) and, for some reason, was interested in this spelling variation enough to make a personal visit to the Tomb of Iymery to study this difference for himself.

But what had prompted Vyse to make this visit to this tomb at such a late date? Was it perhaps that he was up against a deadline, that in just a few days' time a cargo ship bound for London would be setting sail from the port at Alexandria, and Vyse wanted Hill's facsimile drawing of the Khufu cartouche aboard that ship, spelled correctly, of course? If so, then Vyse had to make absolutely sure that the cartouche was correctly written before sending off Hill's facsimile copy of it to London, thus his late visit to the Tomb of Iymery to observe the different Khufu spellings in hopes that they might perhaps be explained.

As noted above, in his journal Vyse writes in the margin of this page on June 16 that the Suphis/Khufu cartouches (observed at the Tomb of Iymery) were different from the Suphis/Khufu cartouche he had drawn on that same page (fig. 13.4, *top right*) where he writes, "in Campbell's Chamber." However, on June 2 (two weeks earlier) he had actually been sent drawings of the Khufu cartouches from this tomb by Perring, showing striated discs (fig. 13.6). So Vyse had known for two weeks of the differently spelled Khufu cartouches in this tomb.

Why didn't Vyse simply accept Perring's drawings of these Khufu cartouches, which were sent to him on June 2? Did Vyse perhaps think that Perring had made a mistake in his drawings, thereby forcing Vyse to go to this tomb to double-check the spelling of these cartouches for himself? Why would this detail have been so important to Vyse?

In this entry to his journal, Vyse is clearly making a comparison with one set of Khufu/Suphis cartouches (in the Tomb of Iymery) with the Suphis/Khufu cartouche "in Campbell's Chamber" he had drawn on this page of June 16 (fig. 13.4). Indeed, this comparison between cartouche spellings seems to have been the single objective of Vyse's visit to this tomb. Given this particular objective then it is surely reasonable

Fig. 13.6. Khufu cartouches with striated discs from the Tomb of Iymery (Image: Vyse, Operations Carried On at the Pyramids of Gizeh in 1837, *vol. II, 7–8)*

Exhibit 9 • The Journal Speaks 175

to expect that Vyse would, at the very least, have made absolutely sure that he had made an accurate drawing—in every detail—of the cartouche that was "in Campbell's Chamber" on this page of his journal to take with him to the Tomb of Iymery to make his comparison with the other cartouches there. Indeed, making an accurate drawing of the cartouche that was "in Campbell's Chamber" would have been absolutely *essential* to the viability of any comparative study Vyse hoped to make, and, as such, it is simply inconceivable that the colonel would not have made, on this page, an accurate rendering of the Suphis/Khufu cartouche that was, at that time, "in Campbell's Chamber." As such, we are surely obliged to accept that Vyse's drawing of the *plain disc* in the cartouche on this page of his private journal was wholly intended as this is how this disc *was* painted "in Campbell's Chamber" at that time in 1837—with *no* horizontal lines. And it is entirely contrary to what we find in the chamber today.

This comment by Vyse is quite revealing in another way. It stands to reason that if the Suphis/Khufu cartouche "in Campbell's Chamber" already contained a disc with striations (but he had simply overlooked placing the lines within the disc on this page), then Vyse, at this time, would surely not have written in his journal that these cartouches he found in the Tomb of Iymery *with* disc striations (fig. 13.6) were *different* from the Suphis/Khufu "in Campbell's Chamber" but, rather, that they were the *same*.

So, it is with this casual remark in his private journal that Vyse betrays the truth of the situation. In short, if the cartouches at the Tomb of Iymery contained striated discs and were described by Vyse as "different" from the Suphis/Khufu cartouche "in Campbell's Chamber" (copied onto the midpage of his journal), this implies, logically, that the disc of the Suphis/Khufu cartouche in the Great Pyramid must, at that time, have been *blank*—which is not how it appears today.

So, having observed and verified the different spelling of the Suphis/Khufu cartouche disc from the Tomb of Iymery for himself, Vyse now acts; he sets about making the necessary changes. The following diagrams present a proposed sequence of events, of journal entries,

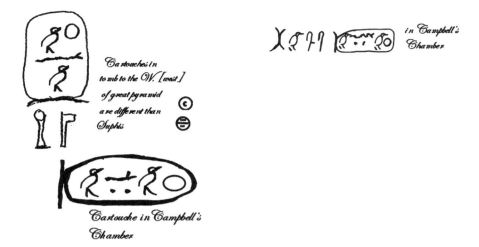

Cartouches in
tomb to the W. [west]
of great pyramid
are different than
Suphis

in Campbell's
Chamber

Cartouche in Campbell's
Chamber

Fig. 13.7. Reproduction of proposed editing sequence of Vyse's journal entry of June 16, 1837. Here we see both horizontal cartouches (master and working copies), both with blank discs and both, naturally, labeled as being in Campbell's Chamber. There is no contradiction between the two horizontal cartouches on the page at this stage of the journal entry. (Image: Scott Creighton, based on original drawing by Colonel Vyse)

edits, and annotations made by Vyse on the June 16 page of his private journal as he learned the truth of the alternative Suphis/Khufu spelling.

First of all, Vyse would have drawn onto this page of his private journal the gang name including the Khufu cartouche (from his master source) with just the plain disc (fig. 13.7, *top right*), writing alongside it "in Campbell's Chamber" (the drawing he would take to the Tomb of Iymery to make his comparative study). We can deduce that this cartouche was likely placed on the page first as it is placed higher up in the main body of the page than the other cartouches (which are drawn in the left margin). We can infer this because the ink used to draw this gang name is much darker than the body text of the page (made with a different pen/ink) and is the same as the darker ink used to draw the cartouches in the page margin, which have clearly been drawn before the main body text of the page as this text wraps around the margin drawings, implying that these drawings were placed onto the page before the main body text.

Exhibit 9 • The Journal Speaks   177

Next, Vyse creates an enlarged *working copy* of his master cartouche in the space at the bottom-left margin of the page; this working copy of the Khufu cartouche will receive many revisions. At this point Vyse copies the disc in the working copy *exactly* as it is in the master (i.e., a disc *without* any of the horizontal lines). Underneath the working copy he writes, "Cartouche in Campbell's Chamber" (fig. 13.7, *bottom left*).

So, at this point there is no contradiction between the two horizontal cartouches on the page as one is merely an enlarged (working copy) version of the other (master), and at this point in his deliberations, this *was* the cartouche in Campbell's Chamber (i.e., with just a plain disc). Note also that at this point all the discs would have been drawn on the journal page with just a *single* disc outline. (There is really no need to draw a disc with a double outline.)

But now, armed with his new information from the Tomb of Iymery, Vyse realizes that this version of the Khufu cartouche is wrong and places a large *X* under his working copy at the bottom of the page, marking it "wrong" (fig. 13.8).

More specifically, however, Vyse then places a small *X* above each of

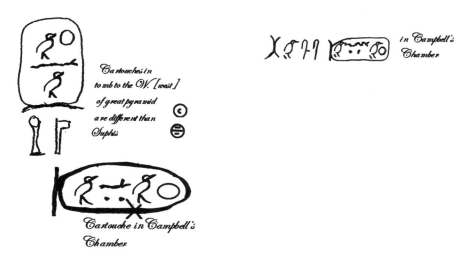

Fig. 13.8. Reproduction of proposed editing sequence of Vyse's journal entry of June 16, 1837. Vyse places an X through the base of his working copy of the Khufu cartouche (bottom left), marking it "wrong." (Image: Scott Creighton, based on original by Colonel Vyse)

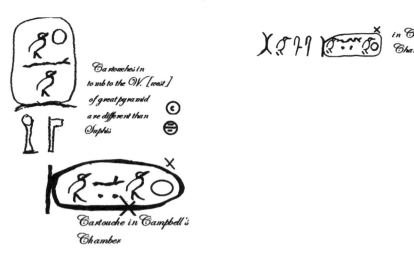

Fig. 13.9. Reproduction of proposed editing sequence of Vyse's journal entry of June 16, 1837. Vyse now places an X above each of the blank discs in his master and working copies of the Khufu cartouche, marking the blank disc "wrong." (Image: Scott Creighton, based on original by Colonel Vyse)

Fig. 13.10. Artist's impression of detail from Vyse's journal entry of June 16, 1837. Close-up of small discs on journal page. (Image: Scott Creighton, based on original by Colonel Vyse)

the plain discs of his master cartouche (fig. 13.9, *top right*) and working-copy cartouche (fig. 13.9, *bottom left*); the blank discs are incomplete and thus "wrong."

For his next edit, Vyse has a decision to make. If we look closely at his private journal page we see that he has drawn two smaller discs (fig. 13.10) just above the working-copy cartouche at the foot of the page.

It appears that the two small discs on this page of Vyse's journal represent what Vyse believed were the only two options that could be placed within the blank disc of his working copy of the Khufu cartouche. But which one should he use? So we observe here another aspect of Vyse's dilemma.

In the Tomb of Iymery we find that there is a vertically drawn Suphis/

Exhibit 9 • The Journal Speaks 179

Khufu cartouche (fig. 13.9, *top left*), with a blank disc. But having now observed Khufu cartouches with the striated discs at this tomb (fig. 13.6, *dashed boxes*), it is conceivable that Vyse would now have believed that the Khufu cartouches with the blank disc he observed in this tomb (and elsewhere) were actually *incomplete discs,* because, in 1837, it was believed (incorrectly) that a blank disc could *only* represent the god Ra, which, by simple deduction, could not then be the correct disc to use for Khufu's name; it had to be a different disc, a disc with internal markings of some kind that would clearly differentiate it from the plain disc of the god Ra.

But what markings should be used? If Vyse believed the blank Suphis/Khufu disc was merely an unfinished disc, what then should be placed within the blank disc to render it the correct spelling for Suphis/Khufu? The upper disc in figure 13.10 appears to show a disc with a partially completed center dot—a circumpunct. Vyse would most surely have known that a disc bearing a center dot was, along with a plain blank disc, also used to represent the god Ra and, as such, could not be the correct disc to use for the spelling of Suphis/Khufu. Deciding this, Vyse then places a small horizontal score through this disc (fig. 13.11), discounting it.

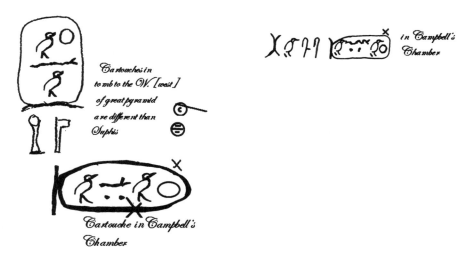

Fig. 13.11. Reproduction of proposed editing sequence of Vyse's journal
entry of June 16, 1837. Vyse places a small stroke through the small
upper disc, discounting it as the correct disc for the Suphis cartouche.
(Image: Scott Creighton, based on original by Colonel Vyse)

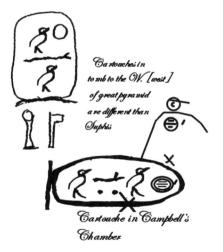

Fig. 13.12. Reproduction of proposed editing sequence of Vyse's journal entry of June 16, 1837. Vyse now places a striated disc inside the blank disc of his working-copy cartouche (lower left). (Image: Scott Creighton, based on original by Colonel Vyse)

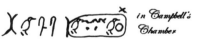

Fig. 13.13. Reproduction of proposed editing sequence of Vyse's journal entry of June 16, 1837. Vyse now "encloses" the striated disc with a curved line and places a small vertical stroke beside the two striated discs, making a cross-reference to his change. (Image: Scott Creighton, based on original by Colonel Vyse)

Exhibit 9 • The Journal Speaks   181

Because the correct disc for the Suphis/Khufu name, according to what Vyse would have understood and believed in 1837, could not be a blank disc or a circumpunct (both of which Vyse would have believed at this time could only represent the god Ra), there was only one option remaining, and Vyse has also drawn this particular disc in his journal entry of June 16, a disc with three stacked lines, which he would have seen somewhere at the Tomb of Iymery (fig. 13.10, *lower disc*).

So now Vyse draws a second disc within the plain circle of his working-copy cartouche, and within this inner disc he places three striation lines (fig. 13.12, *lower left*).

Having now decided which disc to use and drawn this disc inside the hitherto blank disc at the foot of his journal page, Vyse then "encloses" his choice with a curved line and cross-references the change by placing a small stroke beside the two striated discs on the page (fig. 13.13).

The revision of the working-copy cartouche is now complete, and the revised cartouche (now with a lined disc) is ready to be placed in Campbell's Chamber; that is, three lines would now be added to the blank disc in the chamber cartouche (and, of course, a small update made also to Hill's facsimile drawing of the cartouche from May 30 before it is sent to London). It is worth noting here also that in my private discussions with Gorlitz and Erdmann, who, the reader will recall, visited Campbell's Chamber in 2013, they were able to tell me from their observations that the three lines within the disc of the Khufu cartouche have a slightly different color tone from the rest of the cartouche. This tone difference seems to indicate two slightly different paint mixes having been used; that is, one mix made on May 30 and a second mix with a slightly different tone (to add the disc striations) on June 16, 1837.

Having now made all the necessary changes and cross-references, Vyse neglects to remove the legacy and now redundant *X* marks on the journal page. He also neglects to remove or strike out the comment "in Campbell's Chamber" from his master cartouche, although a cartouche with a blank disc is no longer what is actually now present in Campbell's Chamber. After Vyse's modification of the hitherto blank disc, the comment here of "in Campbell's Chamber" now becomes a contradiction. But these are merely legacy marks and comments of a "work in progress"

for Vyse's eyes only. No one except Vyse was ever meant to see this journal page and learn the truth of his last-minute edits, so there would have
been little imperative for him to remove the contradictions, the incriminating evidence, this page of his journal now presents.

There is, however, something of an irony to all of this. Had Vyse
simply kept the plain disc in the cartouche in Campbell's Chamber
(instead of believing that it was perhaps an unfinished striated disc and
changing it), his deception would actually have been far more convincing, because, as previously mentioned, Egyptology now knows that the
plain disc *can* in fact render the name Khufu and that a blank disc does
not always invoke the name of the god Ra. But, as stated earlier, no one
in 1837 fully understood that, so Vyse, in his ignorance of this fact,
must have felt compelled to make absolutely certain of the name by
adding the three lines into the disc, clearly differentiating it from the
plain disc of the god Ra. Vyse, in his ignorance, overegged the pudding.

INSTRUCTING FRAUD

But who would actually place the cartouche (and its later edit) into
Campbell's Chamber, and where exactly was it to be placed? This information presented itself to Louise and me only some time later, after we
became accustomed to reading Vyse's extremely difficult handwriting
style. As indicated earlier in this chapter, around the cartouche drawing
in Vyse's journal entry of May 27, 1837, the colonel writes the following
highly incriminating passage (as shown in fig. 13.14).

> The chamber was 39 long, by 19.10 broad: as it was within "Campbell's
> Chamber May 27, 1837." "For Raven & Hill." These were my marks
> from cartouche [image of cartouche with plain disc] to inscribe over any
> plain, low trussing.[2]

It is, first of all, perhaps worth mentioning here that a trussing is
a triangular support for holding up a structure. The triangular gabled
roof of Campbell's Chamber supports the weight of the pyramid above
and, in this regard, can be considered a trussing. And it is a fact that the

Exhibit 9 • The Journal Speaks 183

Fig. 13.14. Text from Vyse's private journal instructing Raven and Hill to inscribe the Khufu cartouche onto a roof trussing (Image: Scott Creighton)

Khufu gang name with its cartouche is to be found, painted top to bottom, on the lower end of one of the stone roof trussings in this chamber.

Here, then, on this page of Vyse's private journal (from May 27, 1837) we find the colonel making a "note to self" and, in so doing, presenting compelling evidence of a conspiracy to perpetrate a hoax that was to include his assistants Raven and Hill. Note here that Vyse does not make any mention in this passage that he had "discovered a cartouche" on a specific ceiling block when he first entered and examined Campbell's Chamber—something one might reasonably have expected him to write in his private journal if he had indeed made such a historic discovery. Instead, after he signs off this passage with the phrase "as it was in Campbell's Chamber, 27th May 1837," Vyse immediately goes on to write in the very next paragraph of his private journal that he has marks from a cartouche [presumably from his secret cache] that are "For Raven and Hill" *to inscribe* upon the low end of *any* plain trussing. Note that Vyse does not write, "Here are marks from a cartouche I found on a plain, low trussing," which is what one might reasonably have expected him to have written (or something similar) had such an important discovery actually been made during his examination of the chamber.

Vyse does not say here that he found the cartouche *inscribed* (past tense) on a trussing but uses instead the revealing phrase "cartouche to inscribe" (i.e., a cartouche that has yet to be inscribed—future tense). Vyse further states in this brief passage that the cartouche is to be inscribed over the low end of *any* trussing. Vyse does not identify here a *specific* roof block where he had found a cartouche already inscribed (which we might reasonably have expected him to identify were such a cartouche already on a specific roof block) but says, instead, that it is to be inscribed over *any* low trussing. Vyse isn't particularly fussed about which roof block the Khufu cartouche is to be inscribed over and is effectively delegating the choice of the final location, the specific roof block for this inscription, to Raven and Hill.

In short, the Khufu cartouche drawn by Vyse on this page of his private journal was not found in Campbell's Chamber when the chamber was first opened and examined but instead represents the cartouche (from Vyse's master source) that the colonel wanted Raven and Hill *to inscribe* within the chamber, and he also indicated to them where it was to be placed—on the low end of a plain trussing, which is exactly where we find this gang name and its cartouche today.

There is also a hint that when writing this passage Vyse had something of an afterthought. It seems that while Raven and Hill were painting the Khufu cartouche into the chamber Vyse would also have them paint the dedication inscription to Colonel Campbell into the chamber. This may explain why Vyse has placed quotation marks around the phrases "Campbell's Chamber May 27, 1837" (the dedication we find in the chamber today) and "For Raven & Hill." Vyse appears to be linking these two, otherwise unconnected, phrases with the use of quotation marks but only, it appears, as an afterthought, an additional "official" painting task for Raven and Hill to be undertaken while carrying out the primary task of forging the Khufu gang name onto the roof trussing. And, of course, tasked with painting an official dedication into the chamber would provide the forgers with the perfect cover for entering the pyramid laden with pots of paint and brushes to carry out their various painting tasks.

It must be stressed here, however, that Vyse's handwriting is sorely difficult to comprehend and that the above transcript from his private journal of May 27, 1837, is the result of many weeks of studying and analyzing this single passage of text by myself, my wife, and a number of family members, work colleagues, and close friends, as well as a couple of handwriting experts. While it was impossible for anyone to be absolutely certain that the transcription presented above is entirely accurate,

Exhibit 9 • The Journal Speaks 185

all agreed that it is a fair and reasonable transcription of this particular passage from Vyse's journal. In short, we are confident that our reading of this passage is accurate and that any inaccuracy in our reading would be minor and would do little to alter the general meaning and implication of this passage.

WALTER ALLEN VINDICATED

The game-changing significance of this entry in Vyse's private journal should leave no doubt: here we have Vyse, in his private thoughts, casually making a note of an instruction that is to be given by him to two of his main assistants, Raven and Hill, to inscribe the Khufu cartouche (presumably from his master source) onto a plain section of trussing in Campbell's Chamber.

This one line from Vyse's private journal should leave no doubt that the cartouche in Campbell's Chamber was forged by Raven and Hill on Vyse's instruction. But there is another significant aspect to this particular journal entry by Vyse: the inscribing of marks (legitimate and illegitimate) is clearly intended "For Raven & Hill." The reader may recall the written logbook entry of Walter Allen (see chapter 7), who claimed his great-grandfather Humphries Brewer had effectively witnessed the forgery, writing:

> Had dispute with Raven and Hill about painted marks in pyramid. Faint marks were repainted, some were new.[3]

We subsequently learned that author Zecharia Sitchin had identified Vyse, Hill, and (tacitly) Perring as the probable conspirators in his forgery claim, because these men, in Vyse's published book, were clearly the most closely identified with the painted quarry marks. Raven is *never* mentioned anywhere in Vyse's published work in connection with the painted quarry marks except as a witness, along with some others, to the facsimile drawings made of them by Hill, thus why Sitchin, relying only on Vyse's *published* account, failed to identify Raven as having a paintbrush in his hand.

Yet here we have Allen's handed-down account, written by him in 1954 after discussions with some family elders, contradicting Sitchin and identifying the very same men that Vyse himself identifies in this incriminating passage of his private journal. To reiterate: Allen's account, contrary to Sitchin's, independently identified Raven and Hill as the painters of the marks within the Great Pyramid, and we have Vyse, in his very own private journal, *confirming* Allen's independent account, confirming that Raven did indeed have a paintbrush in his hand, along with Hill. Allen's account of his great-grandfather witnessing forgery occurring at the hands of Raven and Hill (on Vyse's instruction) is now surely vindicated.

Further evidence of Raven and Hill's close working relationship in the chambers of the Great Pyramid was discovered in 2014 by Jon Snape, who has analyzed high-resolution photos taken in Campbell's Chamber by French photographer Patrick Chapuis (see chapter 11). In one of Chapuis's photographs, Snape noticed that the two men had placed a little piece of graffiti of their own on one of the granite floor blocks inside Campbell's Chamber, just to the bottom right of the date "1837" in the dedication inscription (fig. 13.15).

Fig. 13.15. Photo of granite floor block from Campbell's Chamber showing Raven and Hill graffiti. The graffiti reads "HRAVEN & Hill." (Image: Patrick Chapuis)

Exhibit 9 • The Journal Speaks   187

It is quite clear, then, that Raven had a close working relationship with Hill in these chambers, a relationship we see on this granite block and of which is evident in Vyse's private journal, but which is entirely absent from Vyse's published account. Could it be that Raven was the person painting the various gang names onto the actual blocks (as instructed by Vyse), with Hill tasked with making copies of Raven's work? Certainly this would ensure that two different hands were at work, two different styles of painting. If this were so, perhaps then Allen's great-grandfather Humphries Brewer had more of an issue with Raven than he did with Hill, and perhaps this was the reason why the colonel ensured that Raven was far removed from any painting of anything (noted only as a witness to Hill's facsimiles) in his published account.

CHAPTER THIRTEEN SUMMARY

- Vyse's private field notes from his time at Giza are held in the Vyse family archive at the Centre for Buckinghamshire Studies, Aylesbury, England. The Vyse manuscript consists of around six hundred foolscap pages. His handwriting, while not impossible, is extremely difficult to read.

- A number of words in Vyse's private journal may be the name Brewer. These have yet to be verified. If verified, then this will categorically prove the story that Humphries Brewer worked with Vyse at the Giza pyramids.

- Vyse writes in his private journal, "Cartouches in tomb to the W. [west] of Great Pyramid are different than Suphis." This indicates that Vyse knew how the Suphis/Khufu cartouche should be written. He could not know something was "different" from the Suphis/Khufu cartouche unless he knew (or believed he knew) how the Suphis/Khufu cartouche should be written.

- Vyse's drawing of the Khufu cartouche in his entry of May 27, 1837, presents the disc with just two parallel dots instead of three striated lines. Text around this cartouche presents an instruction from Vyse to two of his closest assistants, Raven and Hill, to inscribe cartouche marks onto a plain, low trussing (i.e., the roof of Campbell's Chamber). This corroborates the account of Allen, whose great-grandfather Brewer had a dispute with Raven and Hill about painting and repainting marks. Vyse would have had Raven and Hill paint a cartouche (without the horizontal striations in the disc) into Campbell's Chamber around this time.

- Vyse's drawing of the gang name in his entry of June 16, 1837, presents the cartouche disc with no internal markings whatsoever—just a plain blank disc. He has written beside this cartouche the words "in Campbell's Chamber." On this date he *also* presents a Khufu cartouche in the bottom-left margin of the page, now including the three horizontal lines. A number of anomalies and contradictions on this page of his journal indicate a change to the disc in the Khufu cartouche from being a plain blank disc to one containing three horizontal lines. This change was likely precipitated by additional information Vyse received from Perring earlier that month, showing a number of Khufu cartouches from the Tomb of Iymery to the west of the Great Pyramid containing the internal disc striations.

- Vyse would not have known in 1837 that both spellings (i.e., a disc with or without striations) were perfectly valid spellings of Khufu. By feeling compelled to add lines to the blank Suphis/Khufu disc in his master source, Vyse overegged the pudding.

- Raven and Hill demonstrated their close working relationship in these chambers by placing graffiti of their own on one of the floor blocks of Campbell's Chamber, below the dedication inscription.

14

EVIDENCE THAT
DEMANDS A VERDICT

We have seen, throughout this book, many pieces of evidence from a wide range of sources that collectively present a highly compelling case of fraud having been perpetrated by Colonel Howard Vyse and his closest assistants within the Great Pyramid of Giza. We have seen that Vyse had the means, the motive, the key knowledge, and the opportunity to perpetrate such a hoax. Above all else, it has been demonstrated that Vyse possessed the ruthlessness of character to do what needed to be done to achieve his objectives, even if that meant breaking the law and being economical with the truth to cover his tracks.

Taken collectively, the information presented in this book provides a considerable body of evidence to support the view that a fraud was most likely perpetrated by Vyse and his closest assistants within the Great Pyramid in 1837—just as Zecharia Sitchin had first proposed in 1980. The following is a list, in no particular order, of the evidence suggesting the painted marks in the relief chambers of the Great Pyramid are nineteenth-century fakes.

We have Vyse, contrary to its implied discovery in his published account, making no mention in his private journal of finding the gang name and cartouche in Wellington's Chamber (later painted by his assistants J. R. Hill and John S. Perring), a find that would have been historically momentous and would have given Vyse the important discovery he was clearly desperate to make; we have Vyse finding Old Kingdom hieratic number signs that are different from the hieratic number signs found in the small shaft chamber, which is strange considering that the two chambers would have been built around the same time; we have the odd absence of any painted hieratic signs in Davison's Chamber when, from a statistical perspective, we should surely have found some; there's the written instruction in Vyse's private journal to his assistants Henry Raven and Hill "to inscribe" (future tense) a Khufu cartouche at a specific location (a low trussing) in Campbell's Chamber; we have the Khufu cartouche with just a plain disc drawn *twice* in Vyse's private journal; we have what appears to be an "artist's scaling grid" drawn with the Khufu cartouche in Campbell's Chamber; we have Vyse bizarrely copying two dots under the snake sign in the cartouche when all the other paint spots in and around this cartouche on the roof block would surely have told him that the two paint spots he elected to copy were no more significant than any of the many other random paint spots on the roof block; we have traces of paint runnels on the roof block at the bottom right of the cartouche where the paint was thickest and appears to spread laterally along the wall joint; we have Vyse visiting the Tomb of Iymery with the specific purpose of checking the spelling of the Khufu cartouches in this tomb (made known to him by Perring) against a version he had drawn in his journal and labeled "in Campbell's Chamber," and yet Vyse apparently fails to accurately draw the cartouche on his journal page (there are no stacked lines in the disc), and we have to wonder why this would be as accuracy of this particular drawing would have been crucial to his objective of making a comparative spelling analysis at the Tomb of Iymery; we have the series of edits in Vyse's diary as he realized the disc within the Suphis/Khufu cartouche needed to be changed; we have the various sets of quarry marks in the chambers scaled perfectly to fit into the available space between floor and ceiling blocks, indicating in-situ painting; we have markings following the contours of the chambers' floor blocks, again indicating in-situ painting; we have these same marks having seemingly been written onto a stone block in such a way as to prevent the inclusion of the cartouche element of the gang name, demonstrating a total lack of understanding of ancient Egyptian writing convention; one of the gang names appears to have been painted (sideways) across two adjacent wall blocks; we have gang names painted (ostensibly at the quarry) in a horizontal fashion, when this arrangement only became the norm around the Eleventh Dynasty, long after the pyramids were built; we have the inconsistency of Hill's signature on the Khufu gang name facsimile sheets, indicating that this gang name with its associated cartouche was copied from a *horizontal* original; we have signs oriented against normal ancient Egyptian writing convention, having been rotated perpendicular to the known top end of a gabled roof block; we have a dubious drill sign apparently copied incorrectly *eight* times; we have signs whose best hieratic match occurs sometime between Dynasties Eight and Eleven, long after the Great Pyramid was built and these chambers sealed; we have the eyewitness account of Humphries Brewer regarding Raven and Hill repainting faint marks and painting new marks; we have Vyse confirming Raven's involvement in painting marks in his private account, an involvement that is absent from his published account; we have a painted cartouche on a block that, in reality, should have been smeared with lime slurry that "cemented" small pebbles onto the surface of the block, indicating more in-situ painting; we have chemical analysis showing marks painted *sideways* onto a surface of plaster, again suggesting in-situ painting; we have lime slurry running down the wall blocks that magically manage to avoid coating any of the painted quarry marks; we have Vyse giving the impression in his published account that he had no idea that he had discovered any cartouche among the quarry marks found, an impression that is entirely false as it is entirely contradicted by his private account.

And so, by means of deductive, inductive, and abductive reasoning, we have gathered together all of these "dots" of evidence and discovered that they can all be connected logically and seamlessly by one hypothesis—fraud. Some facts presented in this book would be enough on their own to seriously suspect Vyse of having perpetrated a hoax in the Great Pyramid, but it is the sheer weight of evidence, the convergence of facts presented in this book that must surely permit us to seriously question the authenticity of the painted marks in these chambers (*all* of them), as well as Vyse's involvement in their claimed discovery.

In the beginning of this book it was stated that Egyptologists believed (and many still do) that given the complexities of the ancient Egyptian language and the state of knowledge of the language that existed in 1837, it would have been virtually impossible for a layman to have successfully pulled off such a hoax at that time. But from Vyse's private notes we learned that the colonel had a very big advantage, an advantage that considerably shifted the odds very much in his favor, allowing him to succeed in perpetrating a convincing hoax: he knew what the Suphis/Khufu cartouche should look like as it had been published some years before his operations in Egypt began. With that crucial piece of knowledge and a little bit of luck (i.e., finding a Khufu cartouche among a cache of other mainly unintelligible, authentic ancient graffiti), Vyse was set to go. All he needed was to place these so-called quarry marks in a part of the Great Pyramid that no one had ever accessed. And once again the colonel got lucky, discovering and opening four new chambers above Davison's Chamber. Vyse was in the right place at the right time, with just enough of the right knowledge.

In short, the evidence brought forth in this book presents us with the smoking gun that points to a quite audacious hoax having been perpetrated within the Great Pyramid, a hoax that, quite literally, altered the course of world history. With Suphis/Khufu now unequivocally connected to the Great Pyramid via the various royal names that Vyse claimed to have found, the structure was now firmly anchored in the early dynastic period of ancient Egypt, a provenance that is disputed by many independent researchers and writers. Showing that there is a high likelihood that these quarry marks, principally the various royal names, were most probably faked should now allow us to take a more critical view of these marks, of the written word of Vyse, and, of course, of the Great Pyramid's true provenance—Who really built these first giant pyramids, when, and why?

It rather seems that wherever Vyse went and whatever field of human endeavor he operated, the whiff of scandal and of his perpetrating some form of fraud was never too far behind. Indeed, even in Menkaure's pyramid at Giza the odor of a fraud having been perpetrated there by Vyse and his team is almost palpable, whereby the discovery of human remains and a coffin lid bearing the inscription of the pyramid's owner,

Menkaure, was later found to be entirely bogus, the remnants of an intrusive burial from a much later period. As renowned British Egyptologist Sir I. E. S. Edwards writes, "In the original burial chamber, Col. Vyse had discovered some human bones and the lid of a wooden anthropoid coffin inscribed with the name of Mycerinus. This lid, which is now in the British Museum, cannot have been made in the time of Mycerinus, for it is of a pattern not used before the Saite Period. Radiocarbon tests have shown that the bones date from early Christian times."[1]

So what we have here are archaeological artifacts from not one but *two* quite different periods that have somehow magically found themselves together in Menkaure's pyramid, having been "found" by Vyse's team only after some earlier explorers of this pyramid had previously managed to overlook them. Why were the bones and coffin not of the same period? Are we to believe there were *two* intrusive burials from two different periods? Why then haven't we found fragments of a coffin or bones from the *other* intrusive burial (assuming there were two such burials)?

And so we now have to ask: Was Vyse a man in whom we could truly say we can have complete confidence? Can he be considered fully trustworthy, a reliable witness? Is there anything in what we have learned in this book that might raise sufficient doubt about this man that would lead us to question what he claims to have discovered in the Great Pyramid and elsewhere? In legal parlance what we have here is akin to asking: Is there "reasonable suspicion"? Are there sufficient grounds to doubt the veracity of Vyse's published account as it relates to the alleged discovery of these painted marks in the Great Pyramid? In short, are these inscriptions Vyse's greatest gift to world history or his filthiest fraud?

If we take the view that there exists sufficient doubt on the character of Vyse and that there is now also sufficient evidence that casts doubt on his claimed discoveries, how does this impact Egyptology, and where then does Egyptology go from here?

The answer is simple: Egyptology must do what it should have done in the first place with regard to these painted inscriptions—consider them inadmissible evidence until proper scientific tests can be done that will allow us to fully verify their true provenance. Egyptology must now put aside *all* written testimonies made concerning the painted marks in these chambers, including the published work of Vyse and Perring, return to the actual, physical evidence itself—the painted marks—and apply hard science to try to determine the veracity (or otherwise) of these inscriptions, for only then might the truth of these marks finally be settled.

With the authenticity of the pyramid quarry marks in serious doubt, the Great Pyramid becomes a structure that is, once more, largely anonymous to us, and, as such, we can perhaps begin to imagine an entirely different provenance for the monument as well as all the other giant pyramids of ancient Egypt. We can now begin to raise questions that have not been seriously considered since these highly dubious marks and cartouches presented by Vyse from the Great Pyramid effectively silenced the debate almost two hundred years ago: Who were the true builders, and what was the true function of these first pyramids? We can perhaps now begin the process of disentangling and correcting a 180-year-old mistake and take the first tentative steps to discover the true history of these monuments.

And finally, it is not for myself or anyone else to *disprove* the authenticity of the painted marks within these chambers of the Great Pyramid; rather, it is the responsibility of archaeologists and Egyptologists, the custodians of them, to take the issues raised in this book seriously and to set aside their acceptance of the veracity of these marks until better, more scientific evidence becomes available that will help to finally settle this issue one way or another. Egyptology's refusal to see any need to conduct an open and transparent scientific investigation into these markings in the face of mounting evidence that strongly suggests they were faked in 1837 is simply no longer a tenable position. As independent researcher and author the late Alan F. Alford states, "The orthodox argument for the authenticity of the inscriptions is by no means a watertight case. Considerable doubt exists and should be acknowledged."

Genuine or fake—these painted marks within the Great Pyramid have become part of our common history and heritage. The world deserves to know the truth of them.

NOTES

CHAPTER ONE. MAKING HISTORY

1. Kenyon, *Forbidden Science*, 46.
2. Sitchin, *Stairway to Heaven*, 275–76.
3. Sitchin, *Journeys to the Mythical Past*, 23–26.

CHAPTER TWO. SEEKING SUPHIS

1. Sitchin, *Stairway to Heaven*, 272–73.
2. Vyse, *Operations Carried On at Gizeh*, vol. 1, 279.
3. Wilkinson, *Materia Hieroglyphica*, 3.

CHAPTER THREE. MAN OF MEANS

1. Colburn, *Court Journal*, 536.
2. Cottrell, *Mountains of Pharaoh*, 119.
3. Great Britain House of Commons, *Journals of the House of Commons*, vol. 62, 680.
4. Great Britain House of Commons, *Commissioners Report: Elections Beverley*, vol. 18, 387.
5. Ibid., 389.
6. Ibid., 393.
7. Markham, *Nineteenth-Century Parliamentary Elections*, 4.
8. Vyse, *Operations Carried On at Gizeh*, vol. 1, 225.

CHAPTER FOUR.
COLONEL VYSE'S CREATION

1. Vyse, *Operations Carried On at Gizeh,* vol. 1, 107.
2. Ibid., 142.
3. Ibid., 153.
4. Ibid., vol. 2, 156.
5. Ibid., vol. 1, 208.
6. Ibid., 235.
7. Ibid., 61.
8. Ibid., 70.
9. Ibid., 83–84.
10. Cottrell, *Mountains of Pharaoh,* 121.
11. Vyse, *Operations Carried On at Gizeh,* vol. 1, 28.
12. Ibid., 238.

CHAPTER FIVE.
EXHIBIT 1: OTHER CHAMBERS, OTHER TEXTS

1. Walpole, *Memoirs,* xx–xxi.
2. Lorenzi, "Pyramid Hieroglyphs."

CHAPTER SIX.
EXHIBIT 2: THE SILENT JOURNAL

1. Vyse, *Operations Carried On at Gizeh,* vol. 1, 205–7.
2. Stower, "Re: Transcribe This Snippet."

CHAPTER SEVEN. EXHIBIT 3: THE EYEWITNESS

1. Sitchin, *Journeys to the Mythical Past,* 28–29.
2. Ibid., 30.
3. Ibid.
4. Chute, "Her Ancestors Come to Life." *Pittsburgh Post-Gazette.*
5. Lawton and Ogilvie-Herald, *Giza: The Truth,* 107.
6. Vyse, *Operations Carried On at Gizeh,* vol. 2, 152–76.
7. "The Blossburg Coal Mines," *Watkins Express,* August 3, 1865.

8. Sitchin, *Journeys to the Mythical Past,* 31.

9. Sitchin, *Stairway to Heaven,* 277.

CHAPTER EIGHT.
EXHIBIT 4: MYSTERY MARKS MADE IN SITU

1. Reisner, *Mycerinus,* Plan XI (Cheops 88).

2. Ibid., (Cheops 89).

3. Hancock, *Fingerprints of the Gods,* xxxiv–xxxv.

4. Hancock, "Re: Question for Graham."

5. Goedicke, *Old Hieratic Paleography,* P5, Hatnub, 30b.

CHAPTER NINE.
EXHIBIT 5: A PECULIAR DISTRIBUTION

1. Roth, *Egyptian Phyles in the Old Kingdom,* 151.

CHAPTER TEN.
EXHIBIT 6: THE LIE OF THE LANDSCAPES

1. Vyse, *Operations Carried On at Gizeh,* vol. 1, 279, 285.

CHAPTER ELEVEN.
EXHIBIT 7: CARTOUCHE CONTRADICTIONS

1. Hooker, *Reading the Past: Ancient Writing,* 95.

2. Snape, "Re: About Those Two Dots . . ."

3. Ibid.

4. Lamar and Shrode, *Water Soluble Salts,* 100.

5. Mulertt, "Proof of forgery? You decide."

CHAPTER TWELVE. EXHIBIT 8: SIGNS OUT OF TIME

1. Goedicke, *Old Hieratic Paleography,* xiii.

2. Ibid., U24, Heqanachte, 40b.

3. Ibid., P5, Hatnub, 30b.

4. Ibid., G43, Funerary, 17b.

5. Ibid., S42, Hatnub, 36b.

CHAPTER THIRTEEN.
EXHIBIT 9: THE JOURNAL SPEAKS

1. Vyse, Private journal, June 16, 1837.

2. Ibid., May 27, 1837.

3. Sitchin, *Journeys to the Mythical Past,* 30.

CHAPTER FOURTEEN.
EVIDENCE THAT DEMANDS A VERDICT

1. Edwards, *Pyramids of Egypt,* 143.

BIBLIOGRAPHY

Bean, William Wardell. *The Parliamentary Representation of the Six Northern Counties of England.* Hull, England: Charles Henry Barnwell, 1890.

Chute, Eleanor. "Her Ancestors Come to Life," *Pittsburgh Post-Gazette,* March 14, 1977.

Colburn, Henry. *The Court Journal from January to December 1833.* London: C. & W. Reynell, 1833.

Cottrell, Leonard. *The Mountains of Pharaoh.* London: Robert Hale Ltd., 1956.

Edwards, Sir I. E. S. *The Pyramids of Egypt.* London: Penguin Books, 1993.

Goedicke, Hans G. *Old Hieratic Paleography.* Baltimore: Halgo Inc., 1988.

Great Britain House of Commons. *Journals of the House of Commons* 62 (July 1807): 680. HM Stationery Office.

———. "The Existence of Corrupt Practices at the Last Election and at Previous Elections of Members to Sit in Parliament for the Borough of Beverley." *Reports from Commissioners, Great Britain, House of Commons* 18: 1870. HM Stationery Office.

Hancock, Graham. *Fingerprints of the Gods.* London: Mandarin Paperbacks, 1996.

———. "Re: Question for Graham re 'Quarry Marks' in the Relieving Chambers." The Official GrahamHancock.com Forums. www.grahamhancock.com/phorum/read.php?f=1&i=301961&t=301606#reply_301961 (accessed May 25, 2016).

Hooker, J. T. *Reading the Past: Ancient Writing from Cuneiform to the Alphabet.* Avon: University California Press/British Museum, 1990.

Kenyon, Douglas J. *Forbidden Science.* Rochester, Vt.: Bear & Company, 2008.

Lamar, J. E., and Raymond S. Shrode. *Water Soluble Salts in Limestones and Dolomites.* Urbana, Il.: State Geological Survey, 1953.

Lawton, Ian, and Chris Ogilvie-Herald. *Giza: The Truth.* London: Virgin Publishing Ltd., 2000.

Lorenzi, Rossella. "Pyramid Hieroglyphs Likely Engineering Numbers." Discovery News. http://news.discovery.com/history/ancient-egypt/pyramid-hieroglyph -markings-archaeologist-110607.htm (accessed June 20, 2015).

Markham, John, Dr. *Nineteenth-Century Parliamentary Elections in East Yorkshire.* East Yorkshire, England: East Yorkshire Local History Society, 1982.

Mulertt, Audrey, "Proof of Forgery? You Decide . . ." The Official Graham Hancock.com Forums. http://grahamhancock.com/phorum/read.php? 1,343067,343067#msg-343067 (accessed July 16, 2016).

Reisner, George Andrew. *Mycerinus: The Temples of the Third Pyramid at Giza.* Cambridge, Mass.: Harvard University Press, 1931.

Roth, Ann Macy. *Egyptian Phyles in the Old Kingdom: The Evolution of a System of Social Organization.* Chicago: The Oriental Institute, 1991.

Sitchin, Zechariah. *Journeys to the Mythical Past.* Rochester, Vt.: Bear & Company, 2007.

———. *The Stairway to Heaven.* New York: Avon Books, 1980.

Snape, Jon, "Re: About Those Two Dots." The Official GrahamHancock.com Forums. http://grahamhancock.com/phorum/read.php?1,339461,340067 #msg-340067 (accessed July 16, 2016).

———. "Re: About Those Two Dots." The Official GrahamHancock.com Forums. http://grahamhancock.com/phorum/read.php?1,339461,339602 #msg-339602 (accessed July 16, 2016).

Stower, Martin, "Re: Transcribe This Snippet of the VPJ Accurately Thread." The Official GrahamHancock.com Forums. http://grahamhancock.com/ phorum/read.php?1,347875,348001#msg-348001 (accessed July 16, 2016).

Vyse, Colonel Richard William. *Operations Carried On at the Pyramids of Gizeh in 1837.* 3 vols. London: James Fraser, 1840.

———. Private journal. Centre for Buckinghamshire Studies, Aylesbury, England.

Walpole, Robert. *Memoirs Relating to European and Asiatic Turkey.* Vol. 1. London: Longman, 1818.

Watkins Express, "The Blossburg Coal Mines." August 3, 1865.

Wilkinson, John Gardner, Sir. *Materia Hieroglyphica.* Malta: N.p., 1828.

INDEX

Note: **Bold** numbers indicate pages containing illustrations.

BOOKS OF RELATED INTEREST

The Secret Chamber of Osiris
Lost Knowledge of the Sixteen Pyramids
by Scott Creighton
Foreword by Rand Flem-Ath

The Giza Prophecy
the Secret Teachings of the Pyramids
Creighton and Gary Osborn
rd by Graham Hancock

Soul of Ancient Egypt
Spiritual Engine of the World
Bauval and Ahmed Osman

Black Genesis
The Prehistoric Origins of Ancient Egypt
by Robert Bauval and Thomas Brophy, Ph.D.

The Giza Power Plant
Technologies of Ancient Egypt
by Christopher Dunn

Lost Technologies of Ancient Egypt
Advanced Engineering in the Temples of the Pharaohs
by Christopher Dunn

Ancient Egypt 39,000 BCE
The History, Technology, and Philosophy of Civilization X
by Edward F. Malkowski

Aliens in Ancient Egypt
The Brotherhood of the Serpent and the Secrets of the Nile Civilization
by Xaviant Haze

INNER TRADITIONS • BEAR & COMPANY
P.O. Box 388 • Rochester, VT 05767
1-800-246-8648 • www.InnerTraditions.com

Or contact your local bookseller